The Framework of Your Wisconsin Government

2013-2015 EDITION

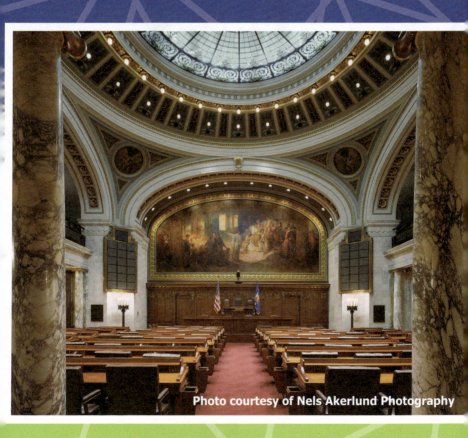

Photo courtesy of Nels Akerlund Photography

A service of the Wisconsin Taxpayers Alliance

Cover photograph: The Wisconsin State Capitol Assembly Chambers in Madison, Wisconsin. Photo courtesy of Nels Akerlund Photography.

The Framework of **Your Wisconsin Government**

© 1955, 1957, 1960, 1962, 1966, 1968, 1972, 1974, 1978, 1981, 1984, 1987, 1991, 1995, 1997, 2001, 2007, 2013
Reproduction with permission only.

ISBN: 978-1-931240-13-0

Wisconsin Taxpayers Alliance
401 North Lawn Ave. • Madison, WI 53704
608.241.9789 • www.wistax.org

Tony Evers, PhD, State Superintendent

An updated, revised 18th edition of the textbook *The Framework of Your Wisconsin Government* by the Wisconsin Taxpayers Alliance is a useful addition to the toolbox of resources that teachers can use to teach state and local government. The Wisconsin Taxpayers Alliance is an independent, non-partisan/non-profit government research group that formed in 1932. The Alliance works to provide objective research-based, accurate, and unbiased information about Wisconsin state and local government. Their emphasis on objective and unbiased information sets the Alliance in a strong position to offer multiple perspectives on the topic of state government. The analysis of bias and multiple perspectives is a valuable social studies skill.

The textbook has always focused on content integration, innovative strategies, and related activities tied to the *Wisconsin Model Academic Standards for Social Studies*. The 18th edition includes technology support such as online resources and PowerPoint presentations for each chapter, which provides strong links to the digital literacy standards included in the *Common Core State Standards for Literacy in All Subjects*.

Wisconsin state statute (s.118.01(2)(c)) requires the teaching of state and local government and basic citizenship skills. *The Framework of Your Wisconsin Government* can assist with these skills as well as meeting state standards in social studies.

The Framework is inquiry-based and offers not only the resources of basic instruction, but also includes opportunities for enrichment, extended readings, and activities that support district requirements for Response to Intervention and differentiation of teaching. The materials reflect an in-depth look at state and local government and the application of knowledge, attitudes, and skills in such areas as state geography and history, economics, the branches of state government and getting involved in local issues. The textbook and supporting materials also offer information about counties, towns, cities and villages, and school districts.

A comprehensive civics and/or government program includes information on state and local government. Educators can use the information in the Framework to align instruction and create curriculum while designing activities that will instill student engagement in state and local politics.

The Department of Public Instruction's Planning Curriculum in Social Studies remains available to districts to provide assistance with curriculum planning related to state and local government in Wisconsin. More information can be found online at http://cal.dpi.wi.gov/cal_socstudies .

Sincerely,

Kristen McDaniel
DPI Social Studies Consultant

Table of Contents

PREFACE 2
ACKNOWLEDGEMENTS 3

CHAPTER ONE
Wisconsin: Its People, Economy, and Government 4
    1.1 A Changing Population 5
        Patterns of State Settlement 5
        Today's Population 5
    1.2 A Changing Economy 7
    1.3 Development of Wisconsin Government 11
        Before Statehood 11
        Developing a Constitution 12
    1.4 Political Thought in Wisconsin 14
        The Era of "Progressive" Reform 15
        Wisconsin's Identity 16
    1.5 Units of Government in Wisconsin 17
        How the Units Fit Together 18

CHAPTER TWO
Political Parties & Elections 20
    2.1 The Role of Political Parties 21
    2.2 Interest Groups and the Media 24
        The News Media 26
    2.3 Casting Your Vote 26

CHAPTER THREE

The State Constitution & the Legislative Branch 30
    3.1 State Governments 31
    3.2 The State Constitution 31
        Wisconsin's Declaration of Rights 32
    3.3 The Legislative Branch 33
        The Legislature 34
        Legislative Leaders 35
        Making New Laws 38

CHAPTER FOUR

The Executive & Judicial Branches 44
    4.1 The Executive Branch 45
        The Governor 45
        Other Executive Officers 47
        State Government Agencies 48
        Current State Departments 49
        Other Departments 51
    4.2 The Judicial Branch 52
        History of the Wisconsin Court System 52
        Wisconsin Supreme Court 53
        Wisconsin Court of Appeals 54
        Wisconsin Circuit Courts 56
        Municipal Courts 57

CHAPTER FIVE

State Budget 60
    5.1 Overview 61

    Magnitude 61
    Other Budget or Two? 61
5.2 The Budget Process 61
    Budget Development 62
    The Legislature's Role 62
5.3 Financing State Government 63
    Taxes 64
    Fees and Charges 65
    Federal Aid 66
    Borrowing 66
5.4 State Expenditures 66
    By Agency 67
    By Purpose 67
    Budget in Action 68
5.5 More Than Just Dollars 70
5.6 The Budget & You 71

CHAPTER SIX

Counties 74
6.1 County's Role and Organization 75
    Differences Among Counties 77
    The County's Dual Role 77
    Organization of County Government 78
    County Board of Supervisors 78
    County Administration 79
    Other County Officials 80
6.2 County Activities and Financing 82
    Health and Human Services 82

Highways 83
Public Safety 83
Financing County Government 84

CHAPTER SEVEN
Cities & Villages 86
   7.1 What are Cities and Villages? 87
   7.2 How Cities and Villages are Created 87
      Boundary Changes 88
      Population Differences 88
      Organizational Differences 89
      City and Village Home Rule 90
   7.3 City and Village Finances 93
      The Budget 94
      The Property Tax 96
   7.4 Putting Property Taxes in Perspective 99
      How Much is $25 Million? 99

CHAPTER EIGHT
Towns 102
   8.1 What is a Town? 103
      Service Problems 105
      Urban Towns 106
   8.2 Powers of the Town 107
      Town Meeting 107
      Town Finances 109

CHAPTER NINE

Education 112
    9.1 School Districts. 113
        State Supervision 113
        Types of Elementary and High School Districts 114
    9.2 Financing Schools 116
    9.3 Alternatives to Public Schools 117
    9.4 Wisconsin Technical College System 118
    9.5 University of Wisconsin System 120

CHAPTER TEN

Getting Involved 122
    10.1 Wisconsin Government & You 123
    10.2 Politics: Democracy in Action 124
    10.3 A Continuum of Political Action 125
        Apathy 125
        Casting an Informed Vote 126
        Taking Direct Action 128
        Run for Office 128
        Civil Disobedience 129

SELECTED RESOURCES 132
INDEX 134

Wisconsin Taxpayers Alliance

The Wisconsin Taxpayers Alliance (WISTAX) is an independent, nonprofit, nonpartisan organization dedicated to promoting good government through citizen education and research since 1932. We believe that an active, informed citizenry is essential for effective, representative government.

We demonstrate this belief by providing Wisconsin voters, civic leaders, teachers, and students with accurate, objective information about how Wisconsin government works, taxes, and spends through print publications, and online and social media. Visit us at www.wistax.org.

We are funded by donations from individuals, firms, and foundations and are not affiliated with any other organization—national, state, or local. We do not lobby or advocate. We take no government money.

Other publications available from WISTAX:

The Wisconsin Taxpayer. An eight-page monthly magazine covering state and local government operations and finance.

Focus. A biweekly, two-page newsletter covering current legislative and state-local developments—from tax reform to state spending trends.

Legislative and Congressional Directory. A 24-page directory issued biennially. Contains maps of Wisconsin congressional, senate, and assembly districts, and contact information for the elected officials representing each district.

MunicipalFacts. An annual 112-page book containing financial and demographic information for Wisconsin's cities and villages.

SchoolFacts. An annual 150-page book containing performance and financial data for each school district in Wisconsin.

Measuring Success: Benchmarks for a Competitive Wisconsin. An annual 48-page report card tracking Wisconsin's competitive position among the states. It examines more than 30 measures of competitiveness—from agricultural income to venture capital, taxes to test scores, and more.

You can learn more about our publications and purchase them at www.wistax.org. □

Preface

Our liberty can never be safe but in the hands of the people themselves, in the hands of the people with a certain degree of instruction.
—Thomas Jefferson

When Thomas Jefferson spoke those words, our country was in its infancy. Wisconsin was not yet a state. He and others recognized that for a democracy to succeed and prosper, its citizens must be educated. That is the work of the Wisconsin Taxpayers Alliance.

When we first published *The Framework of Your Wisconsin Government* in 1955, we were simply trying to fill the need for Wisconsin-specific civics curriculum in our schools. We never dreamed this book would be revised over 18 times in nearly 60 years and be used in middle schools, high schools, technical colleges and universities, prisons, and immigrant training programs.

While the content has changed and the audience has expanded, the WISTAX mission of educating students and aspiring citizens about our government has not.

We still struggle with many of the same issues that confronted our grandparents: How does the community, through its government, answer the needs of society when our financial resources are limited? How do we help educate our children and workers when so much is changing?

If local and state government leaders are to make sound decisions about issues as varied and complex as taxes, education, and health, citizens need to actively participate. We all have a responsibility to study the issues, to vote, and to communicate with our elected officials. But, in order to participate, you need to understand how government works, how and when it makes decisions, and what you can do personally to affect those decisions.

This book aims to help you understand how Wisconsin government is organized, how the levels of government relate to each other, and where to begin if you choose to participate.

As we prepare this latest edition of *Framework*, we are mindful that change never ceases. Wisconsin's schools, economy, and government continually adapt to that change. Even textbooks must change. That's why this 18th edition has an electronic version, as well as supplemental Teacher Tool Kits to provide hands-on activities and real-life simulations of actual government scenarios.

We also urge you to use our website (www.wistax.org) to access our latest research so you have a reliable source of information to help you become and remain an active, involved citizen throughout your life. ☐

Acknowledgments

The 18th edition of *The Framework of Your Wisconsin Government* incorporates the work of our predecessors, the people who conceived of the idea and published earlier versions of this text.

In preparing this edition, the Wisconsin Taxpayers Alliance relied on the work and expertise of many people dedicated to good citizenship and democratic principles: Kristen McDaniel, social studies consultant at the Wisconsin Department of Public Instruction; Nels Akerlund Photography; the photography staff at the Daily Jefferson County Union; Ryan Wilkinson, University of Wisconsin-Milwaukee Director of Clinical Education; Mike Cozzi, photographer; James Gill, Wisconsin Public Broadcasting; Port Washington-Saukville Patch; The Mining Museum and Rollo Jamison Museum of Platteville; Kenosha History Center; Jay Salvo, Wisconsin State Legislature; Wisconsin Legislative Reference Bureau; Wisconsin Supreme Court; Merrimac Communications; Douglas County Historical Society; Fox Valley Technical College; the Hocak Worak; and Professor James R. Kates, University of Wisconsin-Whitewater.

For authoring new sections, contributing content or ideas, compiling data, and reviewing the edited versions, we recognize WISTAX staff: Todd A. Berry, President; Dale Knapp, Research Director; Kate Lindsay, Research Associate; Sandra Mumm, Business Manager; Steve Sansone, Education Coordinator; Megan Sawle, Publications Coordinator; and Sharon Schmeling, Communications Director. ☐

Resources For Teachers

This new edition of *The Framework of Your Wisconsin Government* has several digital Teacher Tool Kits available to enhance classroom instruction.

The Framework Toolkits, which can be customized by teachers, provide: detailed PowerPoints for every chapter; constructivist activities including simulations; quizzes and answer keys; student worksheets; and in-depth supplemental readings. For more information and to order, see Publications at www.wistax.org. ☐

1 Wisconsin
Its People, Economy, and Government

If you were to take a picture of Wisconsin government today, it would be a snapshot frozen in time. However, what that picture looks like now is influenced by state history. To help understand why we have the government we have today, we first explore the early history of the people and the economy of the state.

IN THIS CHAPTER:

- 1.1 A Changing Population (5)
- 1.2 A Changing Economy (7)
- 1.3 Development of Wisconsin Government (11)
- 1.4 Political Thought in Wisconsin (14)
- 1.5 Units of Government in Wisconsin (17)

1.1 A CHANGING POPULATION

Before French fur traders and European settlement of the state, Wisconsin was home to several Native American peoples. These included the Ho-Chunk (also known as Winnebago), Menominee, Ojibwe (or Chippewa, Ojibway, Anishinabe, and Ojibwa), Potawatomi, Fox, and Sauk. Over time, groups of Europeans, first Germans then Norwegians, came to the state. During and after European arrival, other tribes came to and left Wisconsin.

Patterns of State Settlement

Americans from other states and European **immigrants** began settling in Wisconsin in the late 1820s and early 1830s. **Yankees** settled in southeastern Wisconsin and dominated Wisconsin business, culture, and politics for much of the 19th century. Many Americans from southern states settled primarily in southwestern Wisconsin.

Immigrant
One who comes to a new country to take up permanent residence.

Wisconsin aggressively sought European immigrants to help settle the frontier. By 1850, the largest immigrant groups were the Germans, British, Irish, and Scandinavians. By 1860, the foreign-born and their children made up half of our population. By 1890, that figure had risen to 75%. Wisconsin was known as one of the states with the largest immigrant populations in the United States.

Yankees
Early Wisconsin settlers who came from New York and New England.

Germans were the largest foreign-born group in Wisconsin and for years Milwaukee was a "German" city, with German-language newspapers, churches, and social clubs. Indeed, Wisconsin was considered the most "German" state in the nation between the Civil War and World War I. By 1900, Norwegians had become Wisconsin's second largest foreign-born group.

From 1890 through 1920, other immigrants further enriched Wisconsin's ethnic mix. Poles were the largest group of new immigrants in Wisconsin. Others included Italians, Czechs, Slovaks, Serbians, Croatians, Greeks, Russians, and Hungarians.

Today's Population

The 2010 Census counted over 5.6 million people living in Wisconsin. Given the pattern of state settlement, it is not surprising that 86.2% of the population is white. However, as Figure 1.1 on page 8 shows, Wisconsin's minority population has grown from 4.1% of the total in 1970 to 13.8% in 2010.

American Indians were the state's largest minority group from 1890 to 1950. Today, they make up just 1% of the population. There are now 11 tribes with land holdings throughout the state, giving Wisconsin the 16th highest population of American Indians in the U.S. African-Americans have been Wisconsin's largest minority group since 1950. They currently account for 6.3% of the state's population, with heavy concentration in the lakeshore counties of Milwaukee, Racine, and Kenosha. Wisconsin also has increasing numbers of Hispanics and Asians. They constitute 5.9% and 2.3% of the population, respectively.

Latinos are the fastest-growing ethnic group in the state, more than doubling their population between 1990 and 2000. Before 1950, many were recruited from the American southwest to fill labor shortages in manufacturing. Others were **refugees** from the 1910 revolution in Mexico. More recently, many have come as migrant farm workers and stayed when they found permanent work. Hispanic immigrants have made significant contributions to Wisconsin's agricultural and manufacturing industries.

Refugee
Someone seeking a safe place, especially to avoid war or persecution.

Asian populations have also grown. For example, when the U.S. withdrew from the Vietnam War in 1975, the Hmong, who had aided the U.S., were left in the hands of Communists. Many fled to Thailand and later to the United States. After Minnesota and California, Wisconsin has the third-highest Hmong population in the U.S. Communities of Hmong immigrants are prevalent in La Crosse, Sheboygan, Green Bay, Wausau, and Milwaukee.

Wisconsin has about as many different religions as ethnic groups. For much of the state's history, however, Wisconsin has been among the most Catholic and Lutheran states in the nation.

Over time, Wisconsin's population has become increasingly urban. In 1870, less than 20% of the population lived in cities and villages. By 1930, that figure had risen to almost 53%. In 2010, just over 70% of the population lived in urban areas. About 30% of the state's population is further concentrated in Milwaukee, Racine, Waukesha, and Kenosha counties.

Wisconsin's population, like the nation's, is gradually aging. As Figure 1.2 on page 9 shows, Wisconsin's median age has risen from 27 years in 1970 to 38.5 years in 2010. Moreover, the percent of the population 45 years of age and older has increased from 30.6% in 1970 to 41.4% in 2010.

Economy
The system of producing, distributing, and consuming goods and services in a state, region, or nation.

1.2 A CHANGING ECONOMY

Our **economy** has also evolved with the times. Originally, native peoples lived by hunting, fishing, gathering, and **subsistence agriculture**. It was one of those activities—native hunting—that helped spawn the region's first major economic change.

The popularity of fur hats in Europe made fur trading the major industry in the Great Lakes region in the 1600s. The Ojibwe people established villages at points of trade.

Subsistence Agriculture
Farming in which the farmers mainly grow enough food to feed themselves and their families.

Ho-Chunk Nation Powwow. (Photo courtesy of the Hocak Worak.)

Treaty
A contract in writing between two or more political authorities.

Before white settlement, Native Americans also mined lead, copper, and zinc found on the land's surface. Lead was at the center of Wisconsin's first economic boom. Though still part of the Michigan Territory, southwest Wisconsin attracted a flood of lead miners, often from the British Isles. Soon the population growth that came with this boom enabled Wisconsin to gain territory status and, later, statehood.

Land Cession
To give up claim to, or ownership of, specific lands; yielding land to another.

With increasing numbers of immigrants from Europe and the American east coast, demand for land increased. Through the 1836 **Treaty** of Cedars and the **Land Cessions** Treaty of 1837 (known also as the "Pine Tree Treaty"), the U.S. government secured approximately half of the present state of Wisconsin from the Ojibwe, Sioux, and Winnebago Indians. Reports of copper deposits along Lake Superior led the U.S. to acquire more land. The 1842 treaty with the Ojibwe set the stage for a northern Wisconsin boom in copper mining. For a while, Wisconsin led the world in copper production.

In the 1840s transition from territory status to statehood, Wisconsin's economy again changed. The fur trade was dying as silk hats became more popular in Europe and miners were

Figure 1.1

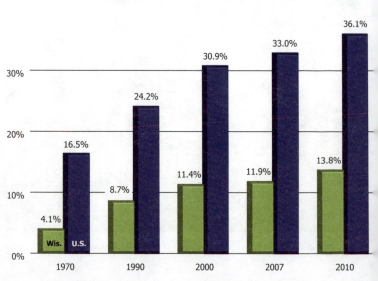

Minority Population: Wisconsin and U.S., 1970-2010

lured to California during the 1849 gold rush. After Indian treaties opened Wisconsin for major white settlement in the 1830s, agriculture became most important. The economy shifted toward grain farming, milling, farm implement manufacturing, and lumbering.

Most frontier settlers were wheat farmers. Wheat farming and milling dominated Wisconsin's economy for about 50 years. In fact, Wisconsin was the nation's leading wheat producer for a few years in the 1860s. During this period, Milwaukee emerged as a milling and shipping center, and several southeastern Wisconsin companies became leading producers of farm implements. Wheat milling remained Wisconsin's leading industry until the late 1880s when lumbering and lumber milling emerged.

The pine forests of northern Wisconsin made the state the nation's leading lumber producer for much of the late 1800s. Between 1840 and 1898, Wisconsin lumber companies cut over 86 billion board feet of lumber. Lumber and timber products topped all other manufactured products in Wisconsin from 1890 through 1910.

Figure 1.2

Age of Wisconsin Population, 1970 and 2010

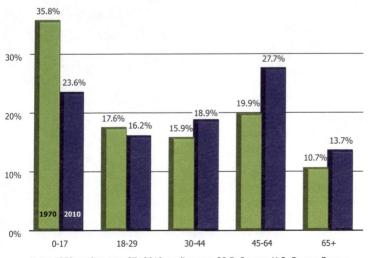

Note: 1970 median age, 27; 2010 median age, 38.5. Source: U.S. Census Bureau

As competition from other states and changes in technology occurred, wheat farming and lumber production declined in Wisconsin. Our economy changed once again. Most farmers eventually turned from wheat to dairy, which was introduced to Wisconsin by New Yorkers and Swiss, German, Dutch, and Scandinavian immigrants. By 1900, dairy farming was Wisconsin's specialty. By 1920, Wisconsin was "America's Dairyland," the nation's leading producer of cheese, butter, milk, and condensed and evaporated milk.

Also by 1920, light industry, such as the production of farm implements, was overtaken by heavy industry in the eastern part of the state. These industries included steel fabrication and manufacture of heavy and electrical machinery, automobiles, and automobile parts. They provided good-paying jobs and became the foundation of Wisconsin's modern economy.

Tourism
The promotion of tourist travel, especially for business purposes.

As the lumber industry faded, wood-related industries, especially pulp and paper production, became important. **Tourism** also emerged as one of the state's largest and fastest-growing industries after World War II.

The Bevans lead mine opened in 1845 in Platteville, Wisconsin. Photo from the collections of The Mining Museum and Rollo Jamison Museum, Platteville.

Today, Wisconsin's economy is based primarily on manufacturing, service, tourism, and **agribusiness**. Wisconsin residents make a living in a variety of other industries. These include insurance, retail, wholesale, mining, brewing, fishing, canning, education, technology, life sciences, and research. Wisconsin's economy continues to change in response to technology and the pressures of worldwide competition.

Agribusiness
Producing and distributing farm commodities, equipment, and supplies.

By 2011, **manufacturing** accounted for 15.8% of Wisconsin's total employment, down from 26.1% in 1970. Yet, because of increased automation and productivity, Wisconsin has remained one of the nation's top manufacturing states. Meanwhile, the service sector has expanded and accounts for nearly one-quarter of all Wisconsin jobs. Small business employment and investment in new, higher-risk businesses, however, trail national averages.

Manufacturing
The process of converting materials into finished goods.

State and local leaders seek to attract and retain a desirable mix of businesses that will provide Wisconsin citizens with good-paying jobs. They realize that a healthy economy generates the income and sales taxes necessary to pay for government services and our quality of life.

1.3 DEVELOPMENT OF WISCONSIN GOVERNMENT

Throughout Wisconsin history, population changes have influenced Wisconsin government. Diverse religious, ethnic, and geographic groups have varying needs for government services and sometimes opposing ideas about the role government should play in people's lives. As our population continues to change, Wisconsin government will also change to meet the needs of citizens.

Before Statehood

The path to statehood began with European settlement by the French in 1634. The land was then transferred to the British by the Treaty of Paris in 1763. The U.S. took control of the territory through the Treaty of Paris in 1783, ending the Revolutionary War. Congress passed the Northwest Ordinance of 1787, which provided a framework for creation of the Northwest Territories (see map on page 14) and a predictable path to statehood. Ohio was the first state created (1803), followed by Indiana (1816), Illinois (1818), Michigan (1837), and Wisconsin (1848).

American Brass Company employees outside the Kenosha plant, circa 1913. Manufacturing continues to be a major part of Wisconsin's economy. (Photo courtesy of Kenosha History Center.)

Developing a Constitution

The structure of Wisconsin's government is outlined in the state constitution. The process of writing and adopting Wisconsin's constitution was difficult. In fact, Wisconsin's first constitution failed at the ballot box.

In April 1846, Wisconsin voters approved a statehood referendum by a six-to-one margin. In August of that year, President James K. Polk signed a federal law authorizing statehood and permitting Wisconsin to draft a state constitution.

Jacksonian Democracy
The political ideas that were predominant around the time of Andrew Jackson's presidency.

Jacksonian Democracy influenced the framers of the Wisconsin constitution. These ideas—named after President Andrew Jackson, a Democrat—dominated American politics during the first half of the 19th century. They included legislative districting by population, majority rule, and rotation of office. They are still a part of our political tradition.

For instance, majority rule is still generally followed in the legislative process, and representation is based on population. We also continue to believe that the majority should have the opportunity to elect most public officials to short terms of office.

Also during the Jacksonian Era, the "common man" gained the right to vote and hold office. Movements for free public schools and for women's rights began.

The first constitutional convention began on October 5, 1846. The 124 delegates were a talented group. Mostly Yankees from New York and New England, their numbers included past and future judges, governors, and lawmakers. Typically, they were young farmers or lawyers influenced by Jacksonian principles. Politically, 103 (83%) of delegates were Democrats.

The 1846 convention began with promise but ended in disaster. Democratic divisions and personality clashes plagued the convention. It was also too large, lacked adequate procedures, and had too many committees (22).

On December 16, 1846, the convention finished its work, and a hard-fought campaign to adopt the constitution began. Opponents attacked the exemption of homestead property from seizure for debts, as well as a provision granting a woman's right to own property in her own name. The selection of judges and **suffrage** were also debated. The convention approved suffrage for white males only, although the question of "Negro suffrage" was submitted to voters separately.

Suffrage
The right to vote.

The 1846 constitution's financial provisions probably guaranteed its failure. Democratic delegates prohibited banks and limited paper money. Farmers and business interests (particularly along Lake Michigan) saw bank credit and paper money as vital to economic development. In April 1847, voters rejected the constitution 20,321 (59%) to 14,116 (41%). "Negro suffrage" was defeated by a similar margin.

With support for statehood still high, a second convention met on December 15, 1847. The new delegates had learned from the first convention. Although still rooted in the northeast U.S., the second convention was smaller (69 delegates), more politically balanced (62% Democrat), had fewer committees (six), and was more disciplined.

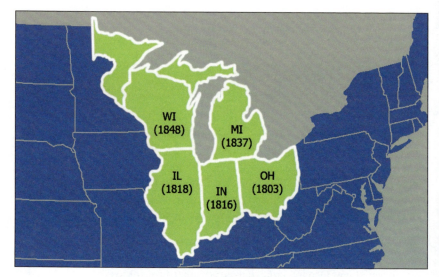

Present-day states created from the Northwest Territory.

Participants were also more careful in handling the controversial issues that doomed the first constitution. The second constitution allowed the legislature to charter banks, subject to voter approval. Property rights for married women and voting rights for black people were omitted, but the legislature was authorized to extend suffrage. The 1848 delegates also bowed to public will, opting for elected rather than appointed judges. In March 1848, voters approved the second version of the state constitution 16,799 to 6,384. On May 29, 1848, Wisconsin was admitted as the 30th state.

1.4 POLITICAL THOUGHT IN WISCONSIN

Together, early Wisconsin settlers influenced two important sets of political ideals that developed in the last half of the 19th century. The first set emphasized the value of personal liberty. Many Wisconsin immigrants, especially those from Norway and northern Germany, wanted to be free from the oppression of their homelands. They opposed government regulation of their personal lives.

These ideals were very compatible with Wisconsin's diverse mix of ethnic groups. Because so many different immigrants settled together in Wisconsin, cultures often clashed, sometimes violently. These problems led citizens to accept a government role in protecting their personal liberty. In time, they learned to accommodate each other.

The second set of ideals that influenced political thought in Wisconsin emphasized education and a positive role for government. Through the "social gospel movement," which influenced university leaders and early **Progressives**, the religious beliefs of the Yankees and other immigrant groups had a particular effect on this way of thinking.

Progressives
Originally a faction of the Wisconsin Republican Party competing with the more conservative Stalwarts for party control.

The last half of the 19th century was a time of great reform in Europe. Many German and Norwegian immigrants knew of the latest European thinking on **government reform.** They believed citizens should work together for the common good. They also believed the strong and powerful in society should be responsible for the weak, and government should help regulate economic life. This belief motivated the start of programs such as worker's compensation and the graduated income tax.

The Era of "Progressive" Reform

Wisconsin political thought provided Wisconsin Progressives and Socialists with fertile ground for their government-reform ideas. The Progressives were a faction of the Republican Party competing against the more conservative Stalwarts. They emerged under the leadership of Robert M. "Fighting Bob" La Follette in the late 1880s. The Stalwarts represented Wisconsin's major business interests (railroads, banks, and manufacturing) that controlled the Republican Party until 1900. La Follette wanted to take control of the party. He promoted open, honest, and free government, and battled against Stalwart corruption in government. La Follette served as Wisconsin's governor from 1900 to 1906, and as U.S. senator from 1906 to 1925.

Government Reform
Change or improvement in government accomplished by altering its form or removing faults or abuses.

Like the Progressives, Socialists believed in using government to improve the lives of all citizens. They had strong German support in Milwaukee. Around the turn of the 20th century, they became a power in the city, and continued to elect some of the city's mayors into the 1950s. Sometimes called **"Sewer Socialists**," they were known for honest and efficient local government. Milwaukee also sent Socialists to the state

Sewer Socialists
Milwaukee Socialists who wanted clean streets, a new sanitation system, and city-owned water and power.

legislature. Between 1902 and 1932, Social Democrat and Socialist candidates for president and governor garnered significant numbers of state votes, sometimes over 10% of the total.

The Progressives and the Socialists cooperated to reform government in Wisconsin. Most of these reforms occurred between 1900 (La Follette's election as governor) and 1915. In 1904, Wisconsin became the first state to enact a direct primary law for nominating candidates for partisan office. Prior to that time, candidates were selected at caucuses or conventions made up of delegates, eligible voters, or members of a political party. This reform was widely viewed as an attack on the Republican Party's closed system of nominating party candidates.

In 1911, Wisconsin became the first state to enact a state income tax, and its worker's compensation law, also enacted in 1911, became a model for the nation. Progressive legislation on factory safety, natural resource conservation, and highway construction was also enacted during this period.

Wisconsin Idea
Using University of Wisconsin resources to provide practical assistance to the people of the state, regardless of location.

Meanwhile, state and University of Wisconsin leaders developed the **Wisconsin Idea** to expand education across Wisconsin. They supported university services to state and local government to create educational partnerships to assist citizens across the state.

Wisconsin's Identity

Although Wisconsin's identity is ever-changing, the Wisconsin Idea remains important. Many state residents still believe that government should work to improve the lives of its citizens. They believe in honest and efficient government. Wisconsin also has had a long history of local control, manifested in its large number of local governments.

Wisconsin government is open. Therefore, citizens can participate in their government and follow what their government officials are doing. Wisconsinites still believe that government, in cooperation with the university and private business, should experiment to find solutions to state problems. During the Progressive Era, this experimentation provided Wisconsin with the first direct primary law in the United States, a model worker's compensation law, and a university extension service that took the university's expertise in agriculture, science, and economics into every corner of the state. In recent decades, this experimentation has continued, with welfare reform, school vouchers, and charter schools reinventing the state and local government relationship and developing a "new economy" for Wisconsin's future.

1.5 UNITS OF GOVERNMENT IN WISCONSIN

Each Wisconsin citizen lives within the boundaries of at least six units of government: (1) the nation; (2) the state; (3) a county; (4) a municipal government (town, village, or city); (5) a technical college district; and (6) a school district. The illustration below shows the broad framework of government under which we all live. Wood County (along with three of its municipalities) is used because it is an average-sized Wisconsin county.

True to its founding and traditions, Wisconsin has many government services delivered close to home by local people. As a result, there are over 3,000 separate units of local government in Wisconsin including 72 counties, 1,257 towns, 190

Figure 1.3

Governmental Units in the State

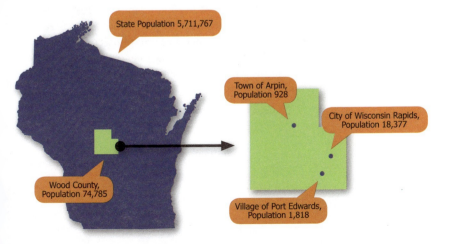

> ### What about tribes?
>
> Tribes remain "sovereign" under federal law. There are 11 federally recognized tribes in Wisconsin today. Each Wisconsin tribe has a government with its own constitution, leaders, and laws. Tribal governments work regularly with federal, state, and local governments on issues of mutual concern.

Special Purpose District
District that provides highly specialized services.

cities, 404 villages, 424 school districts, 16 technical college districts, and 12 Cooperative Education Service Agency (CESA) districts. In addition, there are **special purpose districts** in Wisconsin such as lake rehabilitation, sewerage, and entertainment districts. Some local governments are organized for general purposes and others for a special purpose. For example, towns, villages, and cities provide a variety of services to their residents, such as police and fire protection, while school districts provide education.

How the Units Fit Together

Many people see the various units and levels of government as fitting together much like the layers of a cake. But, reality is much different. The units are not so separate and distinct. In fact, many of society's problems call for cooperation among national, state, and local governments. Therefore, it might be best to think of the units of government not as a layer cake, but rather as a marble cake, with layers that blend and overlap.

Highway construction is a good example. Most highways are built and maintained by state government. Local governments assist the state, sometimes providing construction and maintenance help in return for state financial aid. The national government provides a substantial portion of the money to build major highways.

REVIEW

The framework of Wisconsin's government was developed in the mid-1800s, influenced by New Englanders, New Yorkers, and European immigrants. Wisconsin government changed due to the rise of the Progressives and Socialists in the early 1900s. Government here will continue to evolve as Wisconsin's people and economy change over time. ☐

Key Terms in This Chapter

- Immigrant
- Yankees
- Refugee
- Economy
- Subsistence Agriculture
- Treaty
- Land Cession
- Tourism
- Agribusiness
- Manufacturing
- Jacksonian Democracy
- Suffrage
- Progressives
- Government Reform
- Sewer Socialists
- Wisconsin Idea
- Special Purpose District

2 Political Parties & Elections

Democracy often involves disagreement and debate over the role of government: should it be active or should its role be more limited? Elections help frame that debate. Political parties, interest groups, and the media all play a part in the electoral process. However, citizens have the most important role, voting for the candidates they feel best represent their interests.

IN THIS CHAPTER:

- 2.1 The Role of Political Parties (21)
- 2.2 Interest Groups and the Media (24)
- 2.3 Casting Your Vote (26)

2.1 THE ROLE OF POLITICAL PARTIES

There are two major **political parties** in Wisconsin, the Democratic and the Republican parties. Others that have recently appeared on the ballot are the Greens and the Libertarians. In theory, by voting for the candidates of one party rather than another, you are supporting that party's ideas about what government should do.

Some people cast most of their votes according to the party ticket on which a candidate runs because they expect the official to carry out the wishes of their party. Others prefer to vote for the person and not the party. They think the individual's personality, training, and experience are more important than a party's goals in determining the future action of the officeholder.

Political parties are most important at the state and national levels. The president, U.S. Congress, state legislature, governor, lieutenant governor, secretary of state, treasurer, and attorney general are all chosen on a **partisan** (party) basis. **General elections** are held on the Tuesday after the first Monday in November in even-numbered years.

Party influence is not as important at the local level. Although some county officials, such as the county clerk, clerk of courts,

> **Political Parties**
> Groups organized to influence government elections and promote ideas.

> **Partisan**
> Candidates who represent a particular political party.

Wisconsin's "Open" Primary

In 1904, Wisconsin became the first state to enact a direct primary law for nominating candidates for partisan office. Prior to that time, candidates were selected at caucuses or conventions made up of delegates, eligible voters, or members of a political party.

Most states have "closed" primaries in which only party members can vote to choose that party's candidates. For example, only registered Democrats can vote in the Democratic primary. In those states, voters must publicly register their party affiliation in order to receive the ballot of that party.

In our "open" primary system, voters do not have to publicly declare their party affiliation to cast votes for that party. They make that choice in the secrecy of the voting booth. The voter has access to the ballots of all the parties, but can vote on only one party's ballot.

General Election
Election of representatives by constituents to a legislative body.

register of deeds, sheriff, and district attorney are chosen on a partisan ballot in the November general election, most local officials are elected in the **nonpartisan elections** (elections for judicial, municipal, or school board positions where a candidate appears on the ballot without a party label) that are held on the Tuesday after the first Monday in April. They might be members of a political party themselves, but they run without a party label. They set their own campaigns and do not usually receive financial help from a political party.

Nonpartisan Elections
Elections for judicial, municipal, or school board positions where a candidate appears on the ballot without a party label.

County governing bodies (boards of supervisors), county executives, and all officials in Wisconsin towns, villages, and cities are elected on a nonpartisan basis. Judges and school officials, including the state superintendent of public instruction and justices of the state supreme court, are also elected in nonpartisan races.

The **primary election** for nominating candidates for the April (spring) election is held the third Tuesday in February.

The schoolhouse in Ripon, Wisconsin, where the Republican Party began in 1854.

Whom Do We Elect? When?

Partisan offices[1]

WHEN? Primary held the second Tuesday in August* of even-numbered years (except for president).

Election held the Tuesday after the first Monday in November of even-numbered years.

WHO?
- President
- U.S. Senator
- U.S. Representative
- Governor
- Lieutenant Governor
- Secretary of State
- State Treasurer
- State Attorney General
- Representative to State Assembly
- State Senator
- County Clerk
- County Sheriff
- County Treasurer
- Clerk of Circuit Court
- District Attorney
- Register of Deeds
- County Coroner[2]
- County Surveyor[3]

Nonpartisan offices[4]

WHEN? Primary held the third Tuesday in February[5].
Election held the Tuesday after the first Monday in April.

WHO?
- State Superintendent of Public Instruction
- Supreme Court Justice
- Court of Appeals Judge
- Circuit Court Judge
- County Executive
- County Supervisor
- School Board Member
- City Officers (mayor, alderpersons, some clerks)
- Village Officers (board members, some clerks and treasurers)
- Town Officers (board members, some clerks and treasurers)

---

* Changed from September in 2012 to meet federal directives to accommodate overseas voting.
[1] A constitutional amendment adopted April 5, 2005, extends the term of some county offices (county clerk, district attorney, register of deeds, and county treasurer) to four years. Terms of office vary, so only certain offices are voted on each even-numbered year.
[2] Some counties appoint a medical examiner.
[3] Most counties appoint a surveyor.
[4] Terms of office vary, so only certain offices are voted on each year.
[5] If three or more candidates run for state superintendent, county supervisor, any judicial office or certain other offices, a primary must be held. This also applies to those municipalities that have adopted the system of nominating candidates by primary election. The two highest vote getters are then placed on the election ballot.

2.2 INTEREST GROUPS AND THE MEDIA

Primary Election
An election that narrows the field of candidates.

To increase their influence, many individuals join with others who have similar concerns to form organizations commonly called **interest groups**. Interest groups are most concerned with particular issues, while political parties focus first on electing their candidates. Labor unions, business organizations, farmers, teachers, doctors, lawyers, and students are all groups that work for laws that benefit their members' interests.

Interest Groups
Private organizations of like-minded people whose goal is to influence public policy.

These organizations often hire **lobbyists** to promote their views. There are currently almost 800 registered lobbyists in Wisconsin who represent interest groups at the state capitol. Lobbyists try to persuade lawmakers to support the interests of the groups they represent.

The 10 organizations that spent the largest amounts of money on lobbying during the 2011-12 legislative session are shown in Figure 2.1 below. The amounts vary from over $2.4 million spent by Wisconsin State AFL-CIO to $700,096 spent by

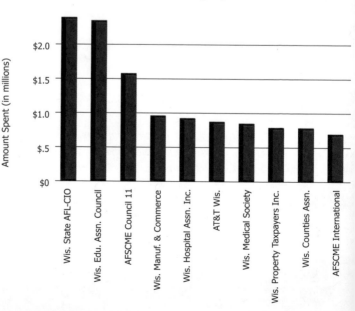

Figure 2.1
Ten Highest Lobbying Spenders in 2011-12

> **Public Records Law**
>
> Unless access is denied by law, any requester has a right to inspect any state or local government record in Wisconsin.
>
> Record is defined in state law as "any material on which written, drawn, printed, spoken, visual, or electromagnetic information is recorded or preserved."
>
> Not every piece of paper or computer file is public record. A draft document is not, for instance. If an authority denies a public records request, it must cite specific and sufficient reason for the denial.

AFSCME International. The types of groups vary from labor unions to local governments. In addition to lobbying, some interest groups routinely make campaign contributions to candidates who support their views. Interest groups may also publicly endorse candidates and encourage group members to work on their election campaigns.

Some people believe "special interests" have too much influence over government decision-making. They worry about money changing hands and political deals being cut. However, "vote buying" is both illegal and rare in Wisconsin.

Others involved in the lawmaking process believe special interests play a key role. One of the major functions of interest groups is representation. Unlike elected officials who represent people in a specific geographic area, interest groups represent people on the basis of shared ideas and help members participate in the political process. Elections are only in the spring and fall, but government decision-making is continuous. Interest groups encourage you to participate more frequently by attending meetings, making phone calls, or writing letters. To see a list of lobbying organizations in Wisconsin, go to https://lobbying.wi.gov/Home/Welcome. You may be surprised at what you find!

Interest groups educate public officials and the general public on complicated issues. Many lobbyists are experts on issues important to their groups. They are key sources of information for lawmakers. Lobbyists often speak at public

Lobbyists
Professionals who represent organized groups seeking to influence legislation or government policy.

Frederica Freyberg conducts an interview on the set of "Here and Now" on Wisconsin Public Television. The media play a significant role in government and politics. (Photo by Jim Gill, courtesy of Wisconsin Public Television.)

hearings. They sometimes do research for legislators and develop ideas for new laws.

The News Media

The media—newspapers, radio, television, websites, and increasingly, social media—play a major role in shaping public opinion. People receive much of their information about government from the media. As a result, lawmakers actively seek to attract attention and to build support for themselves and their ideas. They issue press releases, tweet, and post on blogs and Facebook. The news media also try to influence government through editorial comment on issues and candidate endorsements during election campaigns.

2.3 CASTING YOUR VOTE

U.S. citizens who are 18 or older may vote if they meet certain state requirements. In Wisconsin, you must be a resident of the state and your election district for at least 28 days before the election. In all communities, you have to register before you can vote. This means you must have your name put on the **voter registration** list before voting.

In Wisconsin, you may register at the polls on election day if you have proper identification. Under current law, an elector voting at a polling place or by absentee ballot is not required to present identification other than, if applicable, proof of residence. However, several of Wisconsin's voting laws are under review.

Registering to vote and casting your ballot on election day are not difficult tasks. (You can register online to vote. Go to http://www.gab.wi.gov/voters/first-time.) The most difficult part of your job involves studying the issues and choosing the candidates who will best represent you. This is the best way you can tell your government what you want it to do. Voting is the easiest and most important way to influence your government.

Voting used to be done by paper ballots, but machines have started to replace them. Now most of the counties in the U.S. use optical (56%) or electronic (39%) voting machines. The rest use mixed systems, lever, paper ballot, or punchcard ballot.

Voter Registration
The requirement that voters be registered before being allowed to vote.

Figure 2.2

Voter Turnout in General Elections: 1982-2012

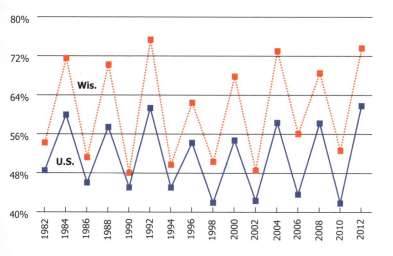

> **How Important Is It to Vote?**
>
> In April 2013, after all the votes were counted on election night, the race for village president in Mazomanie was tied at 201 votes each. There was, however, one absentee ballot that had yet to be counted. When that ballot was counted the following Friday, the incumbent president was reelected by one vote.
>
> In that same spring election, the race for Oregon town chairman ended in a tie. It did not have to end that way, but the voter who cast the last absentee ballot counted chose not to vote in the town chairman race. The race was ultimately decided by a coin flip, with the incumbent retaining his chairmanship. Voting can make a difference!

Voter Turnout
The percent of eligible voters who actually vote.

A higher proportion of Wisconsin citizens vote in presidential elections than those in most states (see Figure 2.2, page 27). In November 2012, 62% of the nation's eligible voters went to the polls during the general election. Wisconsin ranked second in **voter turnout** at 74%.

In November 2010, the Wisconsin turnout was 52.6%. Midterm elections featured contests for U.S. Senate, U.S. House of Representatives, governor, attorney general, state senate, and state assembly—but not for president.

Advisory Referendum
Placing a question on the ballot to measure voter opinion. The results are non-binding.

Tight races often draw more voters to the polls. Also of interest to voters can be special **advisory referendum** questions on local issues.

Only a small number of voters join political parties, communicate with their elected representatives, present their views at public hearings, work on election campaigns, or vote in primaries. When few people actively participate, there is a danger that government of the people, by the people, and for the people will become government of, by, and for the few.

REVIEW

In Wisconsin, partisan elections (those in which public officials are chosen on a party basis) are held in November. Nonpartisan elections (no party labels shown on the ballot) are held in April. Nearly all state elected officials are elected on a partisan basis, while many local officials are elected in nonpartisan elections. Voter turnout in Wisconsin is typically among the highest in the nation. ☐

Key Terms in This Chapter

- Political Parties
- Partisan
- General Election
- Nonpartisan Elections
- Primary Election
- Interest Groups
- Lobbyists
- Voter Registration
- Voter Turnout
- Advisory Referendum

3 The State Constitution & the Legislative Branch

Like the federal government, Wisconsin has three branches of government: legislative, executive, and judicial. Each has specific powers and duties as outlined in the Wisconsin Constitution. To better understand Wisconsin state government, it is important to know more about the state constitution, how laws are made, and by whom.

IN THIS CHAPTER:

- 3.1 State Governments (31)
- 3.2 The State Constitution (31)
- 3.3 The Legislative Branch (33)

3.1 STATE GOVERNMENTS

Not all state governments look the same. In fact, a special feature of state governments in the United States is their variety. Each state has developed a system of government that fits the history and particular desires of its citizens.

All states, however, operate within a federal system established by the U.S. Constitution. The 10th Amendment is particularly important in sorting out federal and state powers. It says, "The powers not delegated to the United States by the Constitution, nor prohibited by it to the States, are reserved to the States respectively, or to the people." These are known as **reserved powers**.

Generally, this means states have any power not specifically given to the federal government in the Constitution. Thus, Wisconsin cannot have its own currency, sign international treaties, or stop interstate commerce, because those powers belong to the federal government. However, Wisconsin and other states have the right to create their own forms of state government, local government (counties, cities, villages, towns, etc.), and public schools.

Reserved Powers
Powers not delegated to the federal government but not prohibited to the states by the U.S. Constitution.

3.2 THE STATE CONSTITUTION

The general workings and organization of state government in Wisconsin are set by the **state constitution**. This document was adopted by the citizens in 1848 as a necessary step for becoming a state, as outlined in the first chapter. You can read the Wisconsin Constitution online at http://legis.wisconsin.gov/rsb/2wiscon.html.

The constitution sets the basic operating rules for state and local governments by describing how these governments

State Constitution
A written document that details the rules, functions, and principles of a state government.

What Wisconsin Can Do Under Its Reserved Powers

- Establish local governments and public schools
- Issue licenses (driver, hunting, fishing, marriage, etc.)
- Regulate business within the state
- Conduct elections (local, state, and federal)
- Provide for public health and safety

are organized and what powers they have. The constitution protects individual liberties and safeguards property rights. It also lists the duties of certain public officials and establishes government finance, taxes, and debt limits.

Each year, new laws are passed. These laws must not violate the constitution. A citizen who questions whether a law is constitutional may take the matter to court. If the court decides there is a conflict, it declares the law unconstitutional. The constitution would then have to be changed before the law could be enacted.

Many states have completely rewritten their constitutions over the years. Though amended many times, the original constitution is still used in Wisconsin. In fact, the state now has one of the oldest constitutions in the nation.

The state constitution can be changed in two ways. One is by **constitutional amendment**. An amendment adds to or changes existing wording of the constitution. Two consecutive legislatures must pass the proposed amendment (the new wording) in identical form. After this, the proposal appears on a statewide ballot and must be approved by a majority of voters.

Constitutional Amendment
A formal change in the existing wording of a constitution.

For example, in 2003, the Right to Fish, Hunt, Trap, and Take Game amendment was added to the constitution in response to increasing attacks by animal rights activists. It added the phrase: "The people have the right to fish, hunt, trap, and take game subject only to reasonable restrictions as prescribed by law." Voters have approved 142 amendments over the years.

Under the other method of changing the constitution, the legislature, upon approval of a majority of the voters in a statewide ballot, can call a **constitutional convention** to revise or rewrite the constitution. This approach has never been used in Wisconsin, although the idea has been suggested.

Constitutional Convention
A gathering for the purpose of writing a new constitution or revising an existing constitution.

Wisconsin's Declaration of Rights

Each state has a bill of rights. In fact, Wisconsin has one of the most complete statements of rights in the nation. Like the U.S. Bill of Rights, **Wisconsin's Declaration of Rights** provides for freedom of speech and the rights to assemble and petition. But, it also prohibits slavery and involuntary servitude, provisions which are not found in the U.S. Bill of Rights.

Wisconsin's Declaration of Rights, which is part of the Wisconsin Constitution, has been amended over the years. For example, in 1967, Article I, Section 23 was added. It requires the state to "provide for the transportation of children to and from any parochial or private school or institution of learning."

Wisconsin's Declaration of Rights
A formal declaration outlining the rights of Wisconsin citizens.

3.3 THE LEGISLATIVE BRANCH

Wisconsin's state government is divided into three branches that reflect three major roles of government. The **legislative branch** makes laws, the executive branch administers laws, and the judicial branch interprets them by settling disagreements over what they mean.

Legislative Branch
The branch of government that is responsible for making the law.

Operationally, these responsibilities are not so clearly divided. At different times, one agency (one part of the executive branch) might have to perform all three functions. Suppose

The Wisconsin State Capitol houses all three branches of Wisconsin state government. (Photo courtesy of the Wisconsin Legislative Reference Bureau.)

the legislature decides there should be safety standards for use of certain machines in a factory. To avoid involvement in technical matters, it may direct an agency (executive branch) to make rules that will have the same force as law (legislative branch). If a factory is charged with a violation, the agency may act like a court (judicial branch) by holding a hearing to decide whether the rules have been violated.

Certain protections exist against an agency using its powers unwisely. Among them is legislative review, which may include a public hearing. Also, an agency's decision about a rule may be appealed to the courts. Finally, the legislature may revoke the agency's authority to make rules or may pass a new law to set aside a rule that has been made.

The Legislature

The legislative branch, the heart of responsive state government, is elected by the people to represent them and to express their will. It has the power to make important decisions that affect the lives of every citizen. This lawmaking power is limited in some ways, however. Constitutional restrictions and the governor's veto power provide some checks.

Redistrict
To change legislative districts to reflect shifts in population.

The Wisconsin Constitution says that members of the legislature must be elected from districts based on population. This means each district should contain about the same number of people. Every 10 years the state legislature uses Census data to **redistrict**.

Senate
The upper house of the Wisconsin Legislature.

The legislature is made up of two separate bodies (or houses), called the **senate** and the **assembly**. The senate has 33 members. Each senator serves a four-year term and is usually elected on a political party ticket from one of the state's 33 senate districts in a November general election. Senators are elected in two groups. Those in even-numbered districts are elected together; those in odd-numbered districts are elected two years later. This allows the terms of office to overlap so that about half of the senators are elected every two years.

Assembly
The lower house of the Wisconsin Legislature.

The assembly is composed of 99 members called representatives. Each representative is elected in the November general election from a single district. Every assembly candidate runs for a two-year term of office, usually on a party ticket. (Each senate district contains three assembly districts.)

A legislator elected in November is sworn into office in January when the legislature convenes. The legislature meets during its biennial (two-year) session according to a work schedule agreed upon by both houses. Sessions of the legislature are identified by the odd-numbered years. Thus, we refer to the legislature that meets in 2011 and 2012 as the 2011 Legislature.

In the 2013 Legislature, the average age of the legislators was 49 years for representatives and 57 for senators. Most legislators had university or technical college degrees. In the 2013 Legislature, one had a PhD, one had an MD, 15 had law degrees, 21 had master's degrees, 60 had bachelor's degrees, and two had associate degrees. They also came from a variety of occupational backgrounds (e.g., 11 were practicing attorneys and 47 listed themselves as "full-time legislators"). Additional occupations included farmer, electrician, physician, forester, and librarian. In 2013, women occupied 33 seats in the legislature.

In 2013, Wisconsin legislators received an annual salary of $49,943. In addition, legislators who live outside of Dane County, where the capital is located, received $88 per day while they were in Dane County on state business. The Madison-area delegation received $44 per day for expenses.

Political parties play an important role in the legislature. In the two houses, legislators organize to do business by party. This type of working group, known as a **party caucus**, includes all party members in the house.

You can search for your legislator at: http://legis.wisconsin.gov/Pages/waml.aspx.

Legislative Leaders

By majority vote, each house selects a chief presiding officer. The assembly chooses a **speaker** and the senate a **president**. In addition, the assembly chooses a speaker pro tempore to preside in the speaker's absence, and the senate elects a president pro tempore. (Pro tempore is an official title that means for the time being.) Although technically elected by

Party Caucus
A meeting of political party members within a house of the legislature to discuss issues or party strategy.

Speaker of the Assembly
The representative chosen to serve as the chief presiding officer of the assembly.

President of the Senate
The senator chosen to serve as the chief presiding officer of the senate.

the entire membership of each house, the presiding officer is really elected by the majority party caucus (all members of the majority party) of each house. Therefore, the presiding officer is almost always a member of the majority party.

The presiding officer acts as chairperson for the day-to-day meetings of the legislature. As presiding officer, both the speaker and the president have the power to interpret house rules and to make rulings, which generally favor their interests. They also determine which representatives or senators can speak on the floor.

Majority Leader
The floor leader for the majority party in each house.

The assembly speaker has been called the second most powerful person in state government, the governor being first. As leader of the majority party in the assembly, the speaker has a large power base. He or she appoints all representatives to assembly committees, including those from the minority party (upon nomination by the minority leader), and determines who will chair each committee. The speaker also assigns bills to committees and controls when they will be debated on the floor.

Minority Leader
The floor leader for the minority party in each house.

Party caucuses in each house select a floor leader, an assistant leader, and a caucus chair. The floor leader for the majority party in each house is called the **majority leader**. The **minority leader** leads the minority party. As party leaders, these officers coordinate their parties' activities in their house during the legislative session.

Changes in Terms, Number of Legislators

Originally, members of the assembly served one-year terms, while state senators served for two years. An 1881 constitutional amendment doubled these terms to the current two years for assembly members and four years for state senators.

The first Wisconsin State Legislature had 85 members—19 senators and 66 assembly representatives. By 1862, the legislature had grown to its constitutional limits—33 in the senate and 100 in the assembly. The legislature remained a 133-member body until 1973, when the number of representatives to the assembly was reduced to 99 so that each senate district would have three assembly districts.

Who Has the Power?

Passing the state's biennial budget is one of the legislature's most important jobs. There are 132 elected officials (99 assembly representatives and 33 senators) who play a role. Of that, 16 have unique input. They are the members of the Joint Committee on Finance.

This committee is typically viewed as one of the most powerful state finance committees in the nation.

Being appointed to the committee by legislative leaders is considered a plum assignment for any legislator. Assignments often go to those who have shown allegiance to their political party's leaders. If the public is lucky, committee members will also be hard working and smart.

The Joint Committee on Finance has the first crack at the proposed biennial budget once it is introduced by the governor. The committee holds public hearings and reviews the bill, offering amendments that have to be approved by a majority vote of the committee. If one political party controls both houses —and thus the majority of votes on the committee—that party has enormous influence. When done with its review, the committee sends the amended budget to each legislative house for debate and action.

The committee was established by Wisconsin lawmakers in 1911. It started with 14 members—five members of the senate and nine members of the assembly. In 1985, lawmakers expanded it to 16—eight from each house.

The committee's powers have grown over time. Its central function is to review the governor's budget. In addition, the committee reviews all legislative revenue and spending bills, and can adjust the number of staff positions for state agencies.

However, it's the committee's role in developing the state budget that has distinguished it from other states. A 1994 study by the National Conference of State Legislatures said that "Wisconsin's Joint Committee on Finance is the most powerful legislative fiscal committee in the country." The study said in most other states, the state's revenue and expenditures are determined by separate committees involving many more legislators.

The report recommended that Wisconsin increase the size of its committee to involve more legislators. Despite talk over the years by members of both political parties about altering the committee, there has been no real effort to change it.

Assembly leaders of the 2013-14 legislative session: Representative Robin Vos (R-Rochester, left), Speaker of the Assembly, and Representative Peter Barca (D-Kenosha, right), Minority Leader. Legislative leaders have enormous influence over their party members. (Photos courtesy of Jay Salvo, Wisconsin State Legislature photographer.)

Though not as powerful as the assembly speaker, the senate majority leader wields tremendous power in the senate. Like the assembly speaker, he or she has enormous influence over how state money is spent and which legislative proposals move forward. The majority leader determines who will chair each senate committee and appoints a majority of each committee's members. He or she decides which bills will be debated and voted on in the senate. Often, majority party leadership can stop bills from reaching the floor in each house even if support for the legislation is strong.

Bills
A bill is a proposal for a new law.

Frequently during a legislative session, partisan majority and minority caucuses meet in their respective houses to talk about legislative issues and plan party strategy. These meetings are often closed to the public.

Making New Laws

Acts
An act is what a bill is called after it becomes law.

Sometimes as many as 2,000 legislative proposals, called **bills**, are introduced during a single legislative session. Only a few hundred of these become laws, called **acts**. The acts are numbered in order of passage to correspond to the legislature that passes them, for example, "2011 Wisconsin Act 5."

The majority of bills amend, make additions to, delete, or rearrange parts of state law, called the **Wisconsin Statutes**. The statutes contain updated versions of all the laws enacted by the legislature in past sessions. Laws dealing with the same subject are grouped together and numbered. The statutes are revised after each legislative session to reflect all changes made, thereby providing a complete and updated set of current laws.

Wisconsin Statutes
The current laws of the state.

Wisconsin's lawmaking process gives a citizen many opportunities to observe and participate. A bill must go through a number of steps before it finally becomes an act (see Figure 3.1, page 40). First, it is introduced in the senate or assembly and numbered in order, according to the house where it originates (for example, Senate Bill 21 or Assembly Bill 21). Bills may be introduced by individual members of the legislature or by legislative committees.

After introduction, nearly every bill is referred to a standing committee by the presiding officer. Each committee considers bills within its area of authority. For example, a committee on natural resources might handle bills relating to the fishing season or to the state park system. Many bills are given a public hearing by at least one of the many senate or assembly committees. Anyone can go to these hearings and speak for or against a particular bill. If a committee reports a bill to the full house, it will recommend one of the following:

- *Passage* (or **concurrence** if the bill is from the other house) with or without amendments.

- *Indefinite postponement* (or nonconcurrence if the bill is from the other house), which means recommending that the bill be "killed." A bill receiving this recommendation is almost never reported to the floor.

Concurrence
Occurs when there is agreement on a bill from the other house.

If the committee vote is tied, the committee will send the bill to the full house "without recommendation."

Many bills might "die" in committee because no committee action was taken, but on occasion, a house might recall a bill from a committee for floor debate.

Figure 3.1

How a Bill Becomes Law*

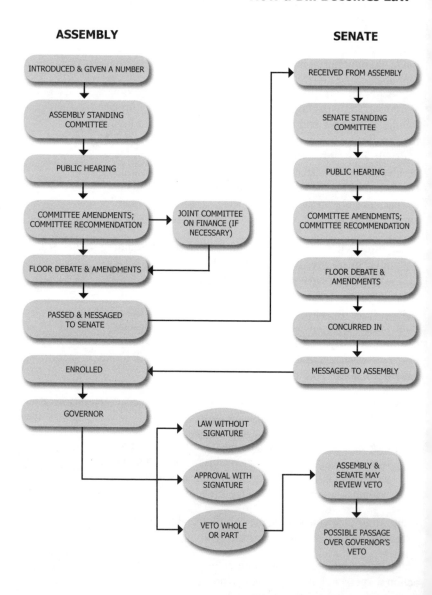

*For purposes of this example, the bill was introduced in the assembly. Bills are also introduced in the senate.

When a bill is reported back to the house with the committee's recommendation, it may be debated by the full membership. During debate, amendments may be submitted by any member. When all amendments, including any recommended for introduction by the committee, have been acted upon, a vote is taken on the bill.

If the bill is passed by a majority vote in the first house, it must then go through the same process in the other house. The second house may concur with the bill as received, amend the bill, or defeat it with a vote of nonconcurrence. If amendments are attached by the second house, the bill must be returned to the house in which it originated so that the amendments may be acted upon.

If the first house does not agree with the amendments adopted by the other house, a **conference committee**, usually consisting of three members from each house, is appointed. The conference committee attempts to resolve the differences between the two houses. After a bill is passed in identical form by both houses, it is sent to the governor for signature. If the governor signs the bill within six days (Sunday excepted) after receiving it, it becomes a new state law. If the governor fails to sign within this required time, the bill becomes "law without signature."

Conference Committee
A committee made up of members from both houses to resolve differences between the versions of a bill passed by each house.

The Joint Committee on Finance working to achieve consensus on differing versions of the state budget bill. (Photo courtesy of Jay Salvo, Wisconsin State Legislature photographer.)

Veto
The governor's action to reject an entire bill passed by the legislature.

Partial Veto
The governor's action to reject a part of an appropriation bill.

The governor may decide to **veto** an entire bill or, if it is an appropriation bill, which spends money (like the state budget), veto part of a bill. In the case of a **partial veto**, the non-vetoed portion of the bill will become law. A vetoed bill (or the vetoed portion of the bill) cannot become law unless the legislature overrides the veto with a two-thirds majority vote in each house.

To track the progress of a bill, learn its legislative history, identify its sponsors, receive a copy of roll call votes on a bill, or listen to "live" debate on a bill, go to Wisconsin's legislative home page at: http://legis.wisconsin.gov/Pages/default.aspx.

REVIEW

Wisconsin's constitution outlines the general framework of Wisconsin state government. In addition to describing the powers of each branch of state government, our constitution also has an extensive Declaration of Rights. The 33-member state senate and 99-member assembly comprise Wisconsin's legislative branch. They write Wisconsin's laws, but are limited by the governor's veto power and judicial review as to the constitutionality of any laws passed. ☐

Key Terms in This Chapter

- Reserved Powers
- State Constitution
- Constitutional Amendment
- Constitutional Convention
- Wisconsin's Declaration of Rights
- Legislative Branch
- Redistrict
- Senate
- Assembly
- Party Caucus
- Speaker of the Assembly
- President of the Senate
- Majority Leader
- Minority Leader
- Bills
- Acts
- Wisconsin Statutes
- Concurrence
- Conference Committee
- Veto
- Partial Veto

4 The Executive & Judicial Branches

While the state legislature creates laws, someone needs to implement and enforce these laws, as well as interpret them and determine whether or not they are constitutional. These are the roles of the executive and judicial branches of Wisconsin state government.

IN THIS CHAPTER:

- 4.1 The Executive Branch (45)
- 4.2 The Judicial Branch (52)

4.1 THE EXECUTIVE BRANCH

Just as the United States has a president, Wisconsin has a **governor**. As the state's chief executive officer, the governor is responsible for administering state government.

To help the governor with day-to-day government operations, the legislature has established about 60 major agencies and departments that make up the **executive branch** (also called the administrative branch) of government.

Though many state employees work in the Madison area, some are also located in district offices, universities, and institutions throughout the state.

The Governor

The governor is elected on a party ticket with the lieutenant governor every four years in the November general election. One of the governor's most important duties is to supervise the state's administrative **agencies** (parts of the executive branch).

> **Governor**
> The executive head of the state government.

> **Executive Branch**
> The branch of government that administers the law.

Governor Scott Walker signing the Concussion Act on April 2, 2012 at Lambeau Field in Green Bay. The Concussion Act's purpose is to protect children under age 19 from critical athletic injuries stemming from multiple concussions. (Photo courtesy of Ryan Wilkinson, University of Wisconsin-Milwaukee Director of Clinical Education and former President of the Wisconsin Athletic Trainers' Association.)

Agencies
Departments and other bodies under the governor's supervision that administer state functions.

It is a difficult job to supervise all state agencies because of the size of state government. The governor is assisted in this task by the officials he or she appoints to head most key agencies. Usually, these appointments must be approved by the senate.

Through these appointments and the **state budget**, the governor exercises power over state agencies. The work of each state agency and the importance of its programs are reviewed every two years when the state budget bill is drafted (written). The governor is required to send the legislature a detailed plan with the amount of money each agency is authorized to spend and the total revenue that must be raised. The budget is introduced as a bill and must be enacted as law by the legislature. The governor has tremendous power at the beginning and the end of the budget process, first recommending the original budget, then using his full and partial veto powers to change or reject the budget bill after the legislature passes it.

State Budget
The plan for collecting and spending the revenue needed to carry out all the functions and tasks of state government.

The governor can also recommend new laws or improvements in existing laws through formal messages to the legislature or through informal discussions with individual senators or representatives. In the past, the governor's power to direct Wisconsin state government was considered weak compared to other states. But changes instituted over time have made Wisconsin's governor one of the most powerful in the nation. Many state agencies previously headed by independent boards or commissions are now directed by officials appointed by, and accountable to, the governor.

Why They Run as a Team

Prior to 1970, candidates for governor and lieutenant governor ran for election separately. A 1969 constitutional amendment provided for the joint election of the governor and lieutenant governor. Why was this change made?

Three times during the 1960s, Wisconsin voters elected a governor and lieutenant governor from different parties. Supporters of the change were concerned about a possible shift in partisan control of the governor's office if the governor died. Also, governors did not want lieutenant governors of different parties acting as governor during the governor's brief absences from the state.

Changes in Executive Branch Terms

Originally, all six executive branch officers in Wisconsin served two-year terms. This began to change in 1902 with a constitutional amendment that increased the term for state superintendent of public instruction to four years. Since the 1970 elections (following a series of constitutional changes in 1967), the governor, lieutenant governor, secretary of state, state treasurer, and attorney general have also had four-year terms.

The legislature has also expanded the governor's authority to appoint top agency officials and has, at times, increased the size of the governor's staff. And, of course, the veto and partial veto give the governor considerable power.

Other Executive Officers

The constitution names five other state officers whom the people elect for four-year terms.

The **lieutenant governor** may take over the duties of the governor temporarily if the latter is out of the state or unable to act. If the governor dies, resigns, or is removed from office, the lieutenant governor becomes governor. A vacancy in the lieutenant governor's office is filled by gubernatorial nomination with the approval of both the senate and the assembly.

Lieutenant Governor
The second highest elected executive officer in state government.

The **secretary of state** has charge of many official state records. If the lieutenant governor's office is vacant, the secretary of state serves as acting governor if the governor is absent or unable to govern and becomes governor if the governor leaves office.

Secretary of State
Elected official charged with keeping record of the official acts of the legislature and executive department of the state.

The **state treasurer** has official charge of the state's funds and administers the state's college savings program. However, state accountants and banks handle most of the day-to-day financial activities.

The **attorney general** is the chief legal officer for the state and its agencies. This responsibility includes advising state, county, and municipal officials on legal questions, and handling most lawsuits involving the state.

State Treasurer
An elected official who serves as the chief banking officer of the state.

> **Open Meetings Law**
>
> Wisconsin recognizes that representative government is "dependent upon an informed electorate." The state's open meetings law ensures that the public shall be notified at least 24 hours in advance of the time, date, place, and subject matter of virtually all meetings of state and local government. Meetings must be held in places reasonably accessible to the public.

The **state superintendent of public instruction** has general supervision of the public schools in the state.

Attorney General
An elected official who heads the state Department of Justice and is the chief legal officer for the state.

With the exception of the superintendent of public instruction, all the above officers are elected on political party tickets.

State Government Agencies

Throughout Wisconsin's years of statehood, the legislature has established agencies to assist the governor in meeting the needs of citizens. (Note: The term "agencies" is a general term referring to boards, offices, commissions, committees, branches of government, systems, and departments under executive supervision.) There are currently about 60 major agencies.

State Superintendent of Public Instruction
An elected official who is responsible for providing leadership for Wisconsin's public school districts.

Agency organization varies. The agency may be directed by a single official called a cabinet secretary, supervised by a part-time board that chooses a secretary or director, or headed by a full-time commission to direct operations.

The usual pattern is to have the agency head (secretary, board, or commission) appointed by the governor with the approval of the senate. Some people argue that it is better to have an agency under the direction of an individual appointed by the governor, because this appointee will be more responsive to the governor's plans and wishes. Others claim a board or commission with overlapping terms is better, because it allows department operations to continue smoothly despite changes in elected officials. Both kinds of organization are used to administer complex state services. Wisconsin's Department of Transportation is directed by a governor-appointed secretary, and the state's utilities are regulated by the full-time, three-member Public Service Commission.

Current State Departments

State departments perform services relating to agriculture, commerce, conservation, education, employment, law enforcement, licensing, health and human services, tourism, and transportation—to name just a few. Activities include such things as collecting state taxes, regulating financial institutions and insurance companies, licensing occupations such as doctors and real estate salespersons, ensuring that food sold to the public is prepared in a sanitary way, and checking complaints about job discrimination.

There currently are 17 departments in the executive branch. The majority of them are headed by a secretary appointed by the governor with the approval of the senate. A brief description of the major ones follows:

Department of Administration (DOA)

The DOA helps the governor prepare the state's proposed budget by providing the governor with needed fiscal information and policy alternatives. In addition, the DOA provides a wide range of support services to other state agencies (such as printing), coordinates various statewide planning activities, and operates the state's buildings, including the state capitol.

Department of Agriculture, Trade, and Consumer Protection (DATCP)

The DATCP serves both producers and consumers. It works to control plant and animal diseases, and it assists producers with information on how to market their products throughout the United States and in foreign countries.

The department is responsible for licensing and inspecting a wide variety of businesses, including bakeries, cheesemakers, food processors, and soft drink manufacturers and distributors. It also seeks to promote fair business competition and to protect consumers and businesses from unfair business practices.

Department of Children and Families (DCF)

The DCF provides or oversees various services to assist children and families, including services to children in need of protection or services for their families, adoption and foster care services, licensing of facilities that care for children, background investigations of child caregivers, and child abuse and neglect investigations.

Department of Corrections (DOC)

The DOC, one of the largest state departments, oversees the care and treatment of adult and juvenile offenders placed under state supervision by the courts. It operates 37 correctional centers and facilities (prisons). The department also supervises convicts on probation, parole, or extended supervision.

Department of Health Services (DHS)

The DHS is responsible for programs relating to public health, mental health, substance abuse, long-term care, services to the disabled, and medical assistance, a health care program for the poor. It works closely with local government units and volunteer agencies to implement many of its programs.

Department of Natural Resources (DNR)

The DNR is responsible for programs relating to air and water pollution control and disposal of solid wastes, such as garbage. It also operates fish hatcheries for stocking state waters, and state nurseries for producing trees and shrubs for wildlife food and cover. Conservation wardens enforce the fishing and hunting laws.

The department oversees Wisconsin's 10 state forests, with approximately 518,650 acres. It also operates almost 50 state parks, eight state recreation areas, and 41 state trails, covering 84,000 acres of hills, valleys, prairies, rivers, beaches, waterfalls, lakes, and more.

Department of Public Instruction (DPI)

The DPI is headed by the state superintendent of public instruction, a constitutional officer who is elected on the nonpartisan spring ballot for a term of four years. The DPI is charged with oversight of the 424 elementary and secondary school districts. The DPI certifies administrators, teachers, and staff. It also administers state and federal aids and provides a broad range of programs and services to schools.

Department of Revenue (DOR)

The DOR administers most state tax laws and collects most state taxes. It also estimates state revenues and economic activity and helps develop tax laws.

Department of Transportation (DOT)

The DOT supervises about 12,743 miles of state and interstate highways. Individual contractors and the counties handle actual construction, repair, and maintenance of these highways, but the state finances them and is responsible for them.

The DOT plans transportation improvements, manages the state's program of transportation aids, and handles land acquisition for rails and airports. It is responsible for 134 public-use airports, 15 commercial ports or harbors, and 3,500 miles of railroad tracks. It assists communities with public transit and pedestrian and biking services. The DOT is responsible for licensing drivers and registering motor vehicles.

Department of Workforce Development (DWD)

The DWD manages Wisconsin Works (W-2), the state's alternative to welfare. It also enforces state laws relating to employment discrimination, equal housing, wages, working conditions, and family and medical leaves. It operates job centers and processes unemployment and worker's compensation claims.

Other Departments

Other departments include: Department of Employee Trust Funds; Department of Financial Institutions; Department of Justice; Department of Military Affairs; Department of Safety and Professional Services; Department of Tourism; Department of Veterans Affairs.

In July 2011, the Wisconsin Department of Commerce was abolished, and the Wisconsin Economic Development Corporation was created. This quasi-independent "department" is governed by a board approved by the senate and headed by the governor. It was formed to develop programs to provide support, expertise, and financial assistance to companies that are investing and creating jobs in Wisconsin and to support new business start-ups and business expansion in Wisconsin.

4.2 THE JUDICIAL BRANCH

Judicial Branch
The branch of government that interprets the law.

The **judicial branch** is probably the least understood of the three branches of government. Although courts attract attention through media coverage of controversial cases, the average individual is most likely to become involved with courts over such things as jury duty, a traffic violation, a divorce proceeding, or the settlement of a deceased relative's estate. To many, the court system appears extremely complicated. Almost every aspect of life is touched by the courts.

Civil Case
A dispute between two or more parties.

Court cases fall into two basic categories. A **civil case** is a dispute between two or more parties, such as when one person sues another in a financial dispute. A **criminal case** is brought by the state against a person accused of a crime (such as robbery, rape, or drug dealing).

History of the Wisconsin Court System

Criminal Case
A case brought by the state against a person accused of a crime.

The basic powers and framework of Wisconsin's court system were established in the Wisconsin Constitution when Wisconsin became a state in 1848. At that time, the court system included a supreme court, circuit courts, courts of probate, and justices of the peace.

Originally, the state was divided into five judicial circuits. The five circuit court judges met at least once a year in Madison as a "supreme court." In 1853, a separate Wisconsin Supreme Court was established with three members chosen in statewide elections and one of them elected as chief justice. In 1877, a constitutional amendment increased the size of the court to five. An 1889 amendment established the current practice of electing all court members as justices and the justice with the

Shirley S. Abrahamson, Chief Justice, Wisconsin Supreme Court, was appointed to the court in August 1976. She was elected to a full term in 1979, and reelected in 1989, 1999, and 2009. She was the first female judge to sit on the high court, and the first female chief justice. Her term expires in 2019. (Photo courtesy of the Wisconsin Supreme Court.)

longest continuous service presiding as chief justice. Since 1903, the constitution has required a court of seven members.

Over the years, the legislature created a complicated network of courts with no uniformity among counties and with overlapping **jurisdictions**. To correct these problems and improve the administration of the courts, the legislature has twice reorganized the court system—first in 1959 and later in 1977-78.

The 1959 law abolished the special statutory courts, established a uniform system of jurisdiction and procedure for all county courts, and established a framework for more efficient administration of the courts. Two 1966 constitutional amendments—abolishing justices of the peace and permitting municipal courts—completed the 1959 reorganization effort. A 1977 constitutional amendment and a 1978 act of the legislature established the system of courts we have today in Wisconsin: the supreme court, the court of appeals, circuit court, and municipal court.

Wisconsin Supreme Court

State law decides which courts will handle which cases (jurisdiction). The **Wisconsin Supreme Court** is the most important court in the state. It has the final word on whether a state law agrees or conflicts with the Wisconsin Constitution. The supreme court is primarily an **appellate court** and serves as Wisconsin's "court of last resort." It also exercises original

> **Jurisdiction**
> The power or authority for a court to hear a certain case and interpret and apply the law in that case.
>
> **Wisconsin Supreme Court**
> The highest court in the State of Wisconsin.
>
> **Appellate Court**
> A court that has the authority to review the judgment of a lower court.

Types of Jurisdiction

There are four kinds of jurisdictions, and courts may hold more than one. They are:

- Original jurisdiction: The right of a court to be the first to hear a case.
- Appellate jurisdiction: The right of a court to review the decisions of a lower court.
- Exclusive jurisdiction: The right of a court to be the only court to hear a case.
- Concurrent jurisdiction: The right of two or more courts to hear certain types of cases, or to handle cases, dealing with the same subject matter.

jurisdiction in a small number of cases of statewide concern and regulates the state's lawyers. The court selects the appeals it will hear, and decisions are final unless federal law is involved.

The supreme court may decide to bypass the appeals court in three instances. First, the supreme court may review a case on its own initiative. Second, it may review a case without an appellate decision if petitioned by one of the parties. Finally, the supreme court may take a case if the court of appeals requests it by a procedure called certification (see Figure 4.1 on page 55).

The supreme court's seven justices are each elected statewide on a nonpartisan basis for 10-year terms. If a justice dies or retires mid-term, the governor may appoint a temporary replacement. The justice with the longest continuous service on the supreme court is entitled to be **chief justice**, but he or she may decline. The 2013 annual salary for supreme court justices is $144,495 and $152,495 for the supreme court chief justice.

Chief Justice
The administrative head of the Wisconsin court system.

The chief justice is the administrative head of the court system. The director of state courts aids the chief justice in managing the judicial system's operations. This organization is much like a corporation, with the chief justice as the chairman of the board, the supreme court as the board of directors, and the director of state courts as the chief operating officer.

Wisconsin Court of Appeals

Court of Appeals
Courts set up to hear cases that are appealed from the circuit courts.

The **court of appeals**, created in 1978, hears cases appealed from the circuit courts. The state is divided into four appellate districts. There is a three-judge panel in one district, a four-judge panel in two districts, and a five-judge panel in the last. Some appeals, such as small claims, municipal ordinance violations, or traffic cases, can be heard by a single appellate judge.

Like the supreme court, the court of appeals takes no testimony. Cases are decided on the trial court record, written briefs, and in a few cases, oral argument. Any citizen may appeal a judgment of a circuit court to the court of appeals. Appellate judges are elected in their respective districts on nonpartisan ballots for six-year terms and their salaries are paid by the state. The 2013 annual salary for appeals court judges is $136,316.

Figure 4.1
How a Case Reaches the State Supreme Court

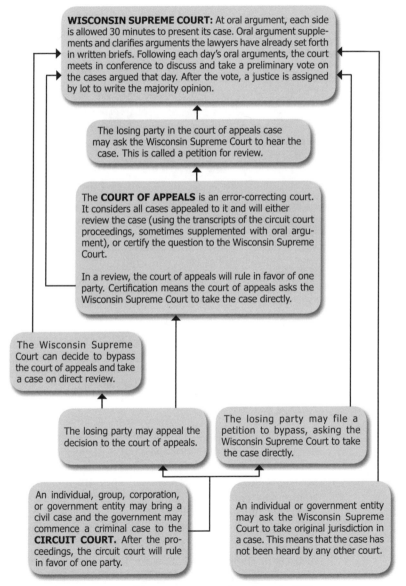

Adapted from a document of the Wisconsin Supreme Court, September 2007.

Juries

The right to a trial by jury is guaranteed by the U.S. Constitution (Sixth Amendment), and by the Wisconsin Constitution (Article I, Section 5). There are three types of juries in Wisconsin: the grand jury, the petit jury (or trial jury), and a coroner's jury.

A grand jury has no fewer than 17 persons and determines if the evidence presented is sufficient to charge a person with a crime.

A petit jury consists of 12 persons in a felony case and six persons in a misdemeanor or civil case. In a criminal case, the jury must render a unanimous verdict to convict, and in a civil case, five-sixths of the jurors must agree to the verdict.

A coroner's jury has six persons who decide if a death occurred naturally or as a result of a suicide or homicide.

Jurors are chosen from the state Department of Transportation driver's license and identification card lists, municipal directories, and utility company lists.

To serve on a jury, a person must be 18, a citizen of the U.S., and able to understand English. If a person has been convicted of a felony, and that person's civil rights have not been restored, he or she may not serve on a jury.

Wisconsin Circuit Courts

Circuit Courts
The main trial courts in the Wisconsin court system.

Below the court of appeals are **circuit courts**, with branches in every county except Buffalo/Pepin, Florence/Forest, and Shawano/Menominee, which share judges. The state has 249 circuit court judges. The 2013 annual salary for a circuit court judge is $128,600.

Circuit courts are trial courts, and they can hear appeals brought to them from municipal courts. These courts are the only state courts to use juries; however, a defendant can waive this right and let the judge decide. They are funded by the state and the counties. For administrative purposes, the circuit courts are divided into 10 judicial administrative districts, each supervised by a chief judge appointed by the state supreme court. Circuit court judges are elected in their respective districts on nonpartisan ballots for six-year terms. The state pays their salaries. The Wisconsin Constitution provides that circuit court judges, like supreme court justices and appellate judges, must be licensed to practice law in Wisconsin for at least five years prior to election or appointment.

Municipal Courts

Towns, villages, and cities may establish **municipal courts** to handle violations of local ordinances. Municipal judges are elected for a term of two to four years. While state law does not require that municipal judges be attorneys, municipalities may impose that requirement. Some municipalities use a joint municipal court in which several local units share one judge.

Municipal Courts
Courts established to try violations of local ordinances.

Figure 4.2

State and Federal Courts and Their Relationship to Each Other in Terms of the Appeal Process

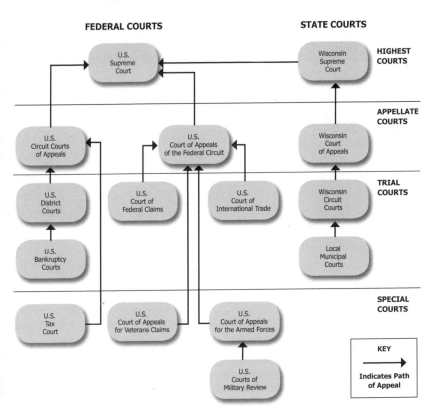

As of May 1, 2011, there were 243 municipal courts and 240 municipal judges in Wisconsin.

These courts have original jurisdiction over violations of city, town, or village ordinances (laws) in the municipality in which they are located. They can levy fines and/or jail according to the guidelines defined in the particular ordinance that was violated.

These courts handle both criminal and civil cases. Criminal cases in municipal courts are only those involving local violations such as traffic offenses, loitering tickets, etc. Civil cases also deal with small amounts of relief. In other words, a person cannot sue for a large amount of money in municipal court.

Decisions of this court may be appealed to the circuit court. Municipal courts do not use juries. If a person demands a jury trial, the case is moved to a circuit court. See Figure 4.2 on page 57 showing overview of the state and federal court systems.

REVIEW

The governor and lieutenant governor, along with the heads and employees of the many state agencies, make up the executive branch of Wisconsin state government. They are charged with implementing and enforcing state law. The judicial branch, which includes the many state courts, interprets laws, and judges their constitutionality. ☐

Key Terms in This Chapter

- Governor
- Executive Branch
- Agencies
- State Budget
- Lieutenant Governor
- Secretary of State
- State Treasurer
- Attorney General
- State Superintendent of Public Instruction
- Judicial Branch
- Civil Case
- Criminal Case
- Jurisdiction
- Wisconsin Supreme Court
- Appellate Court
- Chief Justice
- Court of Appeals
- Circuit Courts
- Municipal Courts

5 State Budget

Wisconsin state government spends more than $34 billion annually and employs nearly 70,000 people, according to the 2013-15 state budget. Since most of that spending is either aid to individuals or local governments, state budgets can be about much more than operating state government. Often, the budget bill includes mandates on schools or local governments, or other policy unrelated to state spending.

IN THIS CHAPTER:

- 5.1 Overview (61)
- 5.2 The Budget Process (61)
- 5.3 Financing State Government (63)
- 5.4 State Expenditures (66)
- 5.5 More Than Just Dollars (70)
- 5.6 The Budget & You (71)

Chapter Five

5.1 OVERVIEW

Wisconsin's **state budget** is a bill proposed by the governor, passed by the legislature, and returned to the governor for signature or veto. The budget is the state's detailed financial plan that covers two fiscal years. Unlike a calendar year that goes from January 1 to December 31, the state's budget year (or **fiscal year**) runs from July 1 to June 30. The fiscal year from July 1, 2011 to June 30, 2012 is called the 2011-12 fiscal year. The state budget covers two fiscal years, or a **biennium**. The 2013-15 state budget outlined taxing and spending for the 2013-14 and 2014-15 fiscal years.

State Budget
A detailed plan of state government spending and how the money for that spending should be raised.

Magnitude

How big is Wisconsin's state budget? The 2013-15 budget authorized the state to spend about $70 billion from all funding sources over two years. That is more than $12,300 for every resident of the state, or $49,200 for every family of four. As will be seen, not all of that is spent on state programs. A significant part of what state government does is to provide financial aid to local governments and schools.

Fiscal Year
12-month period for which an organization plans its budget.

One Budget or Two?

The state has one budget for the two-year biennium. But that budget is made up of several parts, with one part getting the bulk of the attention. The core of the state budget is funded mostly with income, sales, and excise taxes. These taxes, along with several other minor ones, are called general purpose revenues (GPR). The part of the budget funded with these revenues is often referred to as the GPR budget. Much of the focus here will be on the total budget, with revenues coming from many sources other than state taxes, although the concept of GPR will arise throughout the chapter.

Biennium
A 24-month period consisting of two fiscal years.

5.2 THE BUDGET PROCESS

Developing a state budget is no small task. It involves the governor, legislature, and state agencies. The governor submits a budget bill to the legislature in late January or early February of odd-numbered years after the prior year's November elections. While most people view this as the start of the budget process, it really begins more than six months earlier.

Budget Development

In June of the prior year (e.g., June 2012 for the 2013-15 budget), the governor, through the state budget office, issues to all state agencies instructions to be used as they prepare their budget requests. From June through September, agencies develop and then submit budget requests (see Figure 5.1).

The spending requests are the starting point to develop the budget the governor submits to the legislature. The governor also needs to know how much tax revenue will be available in the coming biennium. The first estimate of these collections comes in a November report from the Department of Revenue.

While agency requests provide an initial framework for the state budget, the governor's proposed budget often differs from the requests. Usually, spending requests are higher than estimated tax collections, and the governor has to reduce requests from some or all agencies. Often, the governor also adds new programs in the budget proposal.

Following the January-February release of the governor's budget, the budget bill is officially introduced in the legislature. It then goes to the Joint Committee on Finance (JCF), a committee made up of eight state senators and eight members of the Wisconsin Assembly (see page 37 for more on the JCF).

The Legislature's Role

Acting as the legislature's budget consultant, the Legislative Fiscal Bureau (LFB) prepares detailed summaries of the governor's budget proposals and briefs JCF members. Typically, JCF holds hearings in several locations around the state. The dates and locations are well-publicized. (For current hearings, not necessarily budget hearings, go to: www.legis.state.wi.us.)

If on schedule, JCF works from March until late May or early June, revising the governor's proposal and eventually agreeing on a final bill. Party caucuses are briefed, and the bill goes to each house where it is ultimately adopted. If the two houses disagree, budget differences are reconciled by a conference committee. Once an identical bill is passed by both houses, it returns to the governor for signature or veto. The governor may also veto sections of the bill. Vetoes can be overridden by a two-thirds majority vote in each house.

Revenue
Money collected by state government from taxes, fees, and other sources.

5.3 FINANCING STATE GOVERNMENT

State government relies on several **revenue** sources to pay for spending. In general, they are taxes, fees, and charges; federal revenues; and money received from the sale of bonds (a form of borrowing).

Figure 5.1
The State Budget Cycle

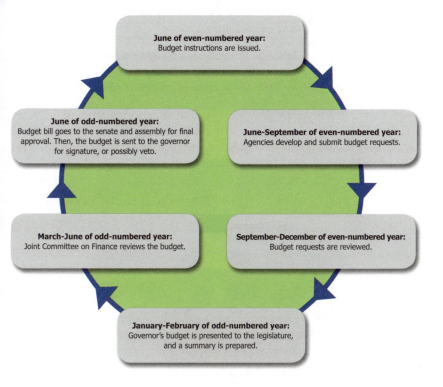

Source: Wisconsin Legislative Fiscal Bureau. Informational Paper 74.
State Budget Process. January, 2013.

Taxes

Most taxes are considered general purpose revenues and can be used to fund any state program. Other taxes are required by law to be used for a specific purpose. For example, the gas tax must be used for transportation; it is not a general purpose revenue.

Individual Income Tax. The individual income tax is levied on money individuals earn from a variety of sources, especially wages and salaries. The state provides income tax forms that individuals use to determine the amount of tax to be paid or refunded, in the case of overpayment. As of 2013, tax rates varied between 4.40% and 7.65%, depending on income. In fiscal year 2012-13, the state collected about $7.4 billion in individual income taxes.

Sales Tax. The state places a 5% tax on the sale of all goods (except groceries and prescription medicines) and some services. In 2012-13, state sales taxes totaled $4.4 billion.

Corporate Income Tax. The state levies a tax of 7.9% on the taxable income of businesses. A total of $945 million in corporate income taxes was collected in 2012-13.

Figure 5.2

Sources of State Tax Revenue

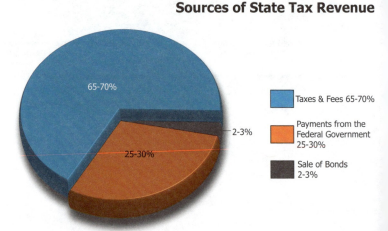

Public Utility Tax. The state levies a tax of 1% to 3% on the gross revenues of utility companies. These taxes generated about $356 million for the state in 2012-13.

Excise Taxes. **Excise taxes** are similar to sales taxes, but are levied on specific items such as cigarettes, other tobacco products, liquor, wine, and beer. They are paid by the seller of the product rather than the buyer. These excise taxes are GPR revenues that collectively generated about $682 million for the state in 2012-13.

Excise Tax
A tax on a specific good or service, often imposed on the quantity purchased rather than the value.

The state also levies excise taxes on gasoline and other motor fuels. These are not GPR taxes. Motor fuel taxes generated about $980 million for transportation projects in 2012-13.

Insurance Premiums Tax. The state generally levies a 2% tax on the premiums insurance companies collect from Wisconsin residents. This tax generated about $150 million for the state in 2012-13.

Miscellaneous Taxes. The state levies other smaller taxes, the largest being the real estate transfer fee paid on real estate sales. Miscellaneous taxes totaled $60 million in 2012-13.

GPR taxes totaled $14.0 billion in 2012-13. In addition, a few state fees are considered general purpose revenues. When these are added to taxes, GPR revenues were more than $14.5 billion in 2012-13.

Fees and Charges

The state collects other revenue through fees or charges for a number of services. The largest is tuition for the colleges and universities that make up the University of Wisconsin System. Other examples include state park or trail stickers, fishing and hunting licenses, driver license and vehicle registration fees, and court fees. These revenues were more than $8 billion in 2012-13.

In budget terms, most fees and charges, along with designated taxes (e.g., the gas tax), are classified as segregated or program revenues. Program revenues are typically user fees for a particular state program, such as university tuition. Segregated revenues are monies designated for specific purposes. The prime example is the gas tax. Program revenues totaled about $4.4 billion in 2012-13; segregated revenues, about $3.8 billion.

Federal Aid

Wisconsin also receives money from the federal government. For example, federal transportation aids help pay for highways. The state's Medicaid program—health insurance for the poor and disabled—is partly paid for with federal assistance. Wisconsin received about $9.5 billion in federal aid in 2012-13.

Borrowing

The state is allowed to borrow money to fund certain projects such as construction of roads and buildings. This is done by the issuing (or selling) of bonds. Revenue from bond sales generally comprises between 2% and 3% of state budget revenues (see Figure 5.2 on page 64).

5.4 STATE EXPENDITURES

What do you think of when someone speaks of state government spending? Many people think of highways, state parks,

Table 5.1

2013-15 State Spending by Agency

Agency	$ Billions	% Total
Health Services	$20.32	29.8%
Public Instruction	12.47	18.3
UW System	11.83	17.3
Transportation	6.03	8.8
Shared Revenues	4.79	7.0
Corrections	2.54	3.7
Children & Families	2.25	3.3
Administration	1.87	2.7
Natural Resources	1.15	1.7
Subtotal	63.25	92.6
All Other	4.98	7.3
Total	68.24	100.0

Note: Figures are rounded.

corrections (prisons), or maybe the University of Wisconsin. Wisconsin state government spends money on these—and more.

By Agency

Table 5.1 shows, by agency, where the state spends its revenues. The **expenditure** figures do not include building projects funded with borrowing. Three agencies combine for more than 65% of state spending.

Expenditure Money spent by state government.

Health Services. The largest part of state spending is done by the Department of Health Services (DHS). In 2013-15, the agency is slated to spend more than $20 billion, or nearly 30% of the total. The bulk of the spending will be for the state's Medicaid program.

Public Instruction. At more than $12 billion, the Department of Public Instruction (DPI) is the second largest spender of state revenues. Nearly all of DPI's spending is state aid to K-12 school districts.

UW System. The University of Wisconsin System will spend nearly $12 billion over the two years, or 17.3% of the total budget. The state also helps fund the state technical college system (not listed). Combined, state funding for K-12 schools, technical colleges, and the UW System makes up about 36% of total state spending.

Others. Remaining agencies account for only 35% of state expenditures. The Department of Transportation has more than $6 billion to spend on various projects, mostly roads and highways. Shared revenues (not an agency) are state aids to municipalities and counties. This category also includes over $2 billion in property tax relief programs. The departments of corrections (prisons), children and families, and administration each claim between 2% and 4% of total spending.

By Purpose

A second way to look at state spending is by purpose. Looked at this way, most state spending goes to helping individuals or helping to pay for local government services.

Aids to Individuals. The state's fastest-growing program is Medicaid, a health insurance program for low-income and disabled residents. It is funded with a combination of federal and state revenues. Medicaid is one example of state assistance to individuals.

Not all state assistance is for low-income people. The state provides some job training and tuition assistance to a variety of individuals. Aids to individuals and organizations represent about 32% of total state spending (see Figure 5.3).

Local Aids. In chapters seven and nine, we will see how local governments and schools are funded partly with property taxes. A second major source of revenue for them is **state aid**. In 2010, state aid accounted for 30% of county revenues, 24% of city revenues, 18% of village revenues, 30% of town revenues, 43% of local school district revenues, and 13% of technical college district revenues.

> **State Aid**
> Money paid by the state to municipalities, counties, school districts, and technical college districts to help finance local services.

The 2013-15 state budget allocates more than $20 billion over two years for aids to local governments and schools. The majority goes to K-12 schools.

Budget in Action

Figure 5.4 on the next page shows the state budget in action. The state collects revenues from the sources discussed earlier—

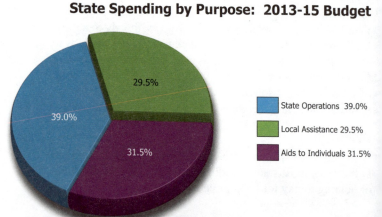

Figure 5.3
State Spending by Purpose: 2013-15 Budget

- State Operations 39.0%
- Local Assistance 29.5%
- Aids to Individuals 31.5%

GPR, the federal government, program fees, segregated fees and taxes, and borrowing. These revenues are distributed to the many agencies.

Agencies then spend those dollars in a variety of ways. Some funds are used to pay for agency operating expenses, e.g., employee wages and benefits; office supplies; vehicle purchase and maintenance. The remainder is used to pay for

Figure 5.4

The Flow of Revenues and Expenditures: 2013-15 Budget

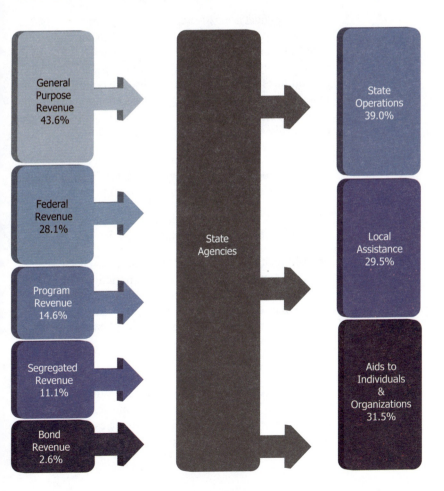

the programs run by the agency. Each expenditure can be broadly classified as either state operations, local assistance, or aid to individuals and organizations.

Each agency is unique in its mix of revenue and where it spends money. Some agencies are funded primarily with GPR revenues, while others receive significant federal support. On the expenditure side of the ledger, some agencies spend nearly all of their revenue on local assistance, while others are focused on aids to individuals.

5.5 MORE THAN JUST DOLLARS

The state budget is mostly about taxing and spending. But dig deeper and you will find there is more to the state budget than dollars. Often, the governor or legislators will include in the budget policy items that have no relation to state revenues or expenditures (nonfiscal items). These are typically included in the budget bill because they get less attention than if they were proposed in a separate bill, and are more likely to pass more easily and quickly.

For example, the governor proposed 57 nonfiscal items in his 2013-15 budget. The Joint Committee on Finance removed some and added others, bringing the total to 93.

These policy items can deal with a wide range of issues. Some examples from the 2013-15 state budget include:

- Eliminating the ability of local governments to require their employees to live in the community;
- Limiting the dates that the Department of Natural Resources can establish an elk hunting season; and
- Requiring the Department of Public Instruction to publish school accountability reports

Mandate
Requirement imposed on local governments by the state.

Some of the policy items and other state budget provisions are **mandates**, or requirements imposed on local governments. State law is filled with local mandates, many of them originating in a budget bill. Some mandates are paid for, at least partially, with state tax dollars. Others are unfunded and less popular with local officials.

5.6 THE BUDGET & YOU

Although you may not know it, the state budget affects you, your family, your school, and your community in many ways.

Budget bills can affect what you learn, what tests are required of you, and how much you pay for college. State educational standards, which describe what the state expects students to learn, are often changed in state budgets. State tests are typically mandated or changed in the state budget. Sometimes, state budget bills restrict tuition increases at state colleges and universities.

Budget bills can affect your school, as well. The 1993-95 state budget imposed limits on the amount of revenue school districts could raise. Each budget since has loosened or tightened those limits. When these revenue limits are tightened, school districts may have to reduce staffing, which could affect class sizes.

Figure 5.5

State Spending From All Revenue Sources

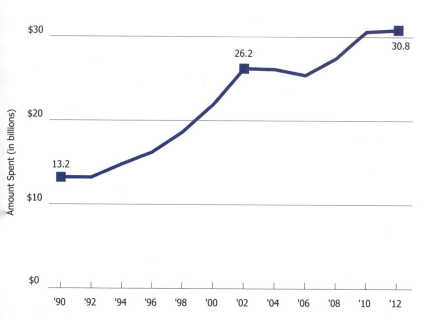

The 2005-07 state budget limited how much counties and municipalities could increase property taxes. Again, these limits were loosened or tightened in subsequent budgets. Like the school limits, these "levy limits" can affect municipal and county services. They can require local governments to provide services more efficiently, but they may also affect services like snow plowing, road repair, and park and recreation programs.

Finally, the state budget affects your family and your household budget. Property tax limits might mean your parents pay less in property taxes or receive reduced services. Income or sales tax increases or reductions mean more or fewer taxes paid to the state. These budget items affect your family's disposable income—the amount your parents have to spend on other things.

The state budget is about more than money, rules, or mandates. Though complex, it affects you, your friends, and neighbors in countless ways and its impact grows over time (see Figure 5.5 on page 71). Knowing something about state taxing and spending is not just for the classroom, it can help you at home, school, or work every day.

REVIEW

The budget process is long and involves the governor, the legislature, and many state employees. State budgets outline revenues and spending for a two-year period. State spending is not just about prisons, roads, and the UW System; a significant part is about financing local governments and schools. Many parts of a state budget affect you, your family, and your community. ☐

Key Terms in This Chapter

- State Budget
- Fiscal Year
- Biennium
- Revenue
- Excise Tax
- Expenditure
- State Aid
- Mandate

6 Counties

The county has always played an important part in Wisconsin government. It was a unit of government even before Wisconsin became a state in 1848. That year, there were only 29 counties. By 1901, the number had grown to 71. In 1961, the newest county of Menominee was created from the territory that made up the Menominee Indian Reservation. This brought the total number of counties to the current 72.

IN THIS CHAPTER:

- 6.1 County's Role and Organization (75)
- 6.2 County Activities and Financing (82)

6.1 COUNTY'S ROLE AND ORGANIZATION

The concept of regional government has been around for a very long time. Saxon kings in seventh-century England divided their lands into "shires." One of the officials serving the king was the "shire-reeve," or sheriff. We still have county sheriffs today.

In medieval France, dukes of Normandy awarded their supporters, called "counts," with land to administer, called "**counties**." When the Normans conquered England in 1066, they brought that system with them. By the early 1200s, shires had been replaced with counties throughout the country.

Counties
The largest unit of local government in Wisconsin.

Early British and French settlement made counties part of the American political landscape. Today, there are over 3,000 counties in the U.S. They may be called "boroughs" in Alaska or "parishes" in Louisiana, but regardless of name, counties remain a way to divide states into smaller areas that can be more effectively managed and governed.

With few exceptions, the form of county government has not changed much since the early days, although the services they provide have expanded greatly. Counties are now an important unit of local government.

Table 6.1

Variations Among Wisconsin Counties (2010)

Land Area		2010 Population	
Square Miles	No. of Counties	Population Group	No. of Counties
Over 1,500	1	Over 500,000	1
1,251-1,500	5	300,001-500,000	2
1,001-1,250	7	100,001-300,000	12
751-1,000	24	50,001-100,000	13
501-750	20	25,001-50,000	18
301-500	11	10,001-25,000	21
300 or less	4	10,000 or less	5

Figure 6.1

Counties in Wisconsin

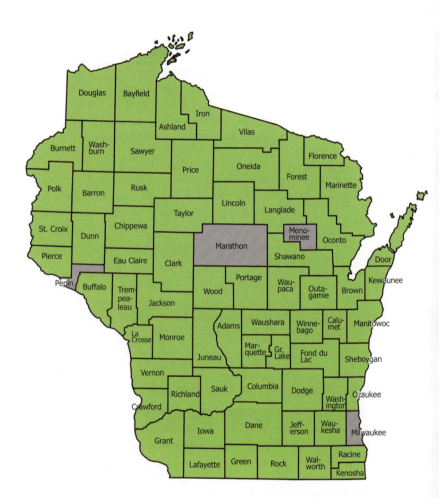

Marathon, the largest county in size, has 1,545 square miles of land area. The smallest county, Pepin, has 232 square miles. Milwaukee is the most populous county with almost 937,000 people. The county with the smallest population is Menominee, which has about 4,600 residents.

Differences Among Counties

One of the problems in discussing or managing Wisconsin counties is that they vary greatly in size and population, as Table 6.1 on page 75 illustrates.

The largest is Marathon at 1,545 square miles; the smallest is Pepin at 232. Wisconsin's most populous county is Milwaukee with almost 937,000 people. Menominee County is Wisconsin's least populous with about 4,600 residents.

Wisconsin counties also differ greatly in their economic resources. Southern Wisconsin is home to rich farmland and dairy herds. Most of Wisconsin's heavy industry is located in the populous areas of southeast Wisconsin and the Fox River Valley (including Brown, Outagamie, and Winnebago counties). Northeast and north central Wisconsin are popular tourist destinations. Northwest Wisconsin also relies on tourism, but the proximity of Minneapolis/St. Paul has also led to growth in the area.

The County's Dual Role

The county serves two purposes. It provides certain services for state government, and it is also a unit of local self-government.

The county is an agent of the state in many ways. The sheriff enforces state laws, including state traffic regulations. The district attorney represents the state in prosecuting those who break its laws. The county highway department maintains the state trunk highways within its borders. The county register of deeds keeps certain records required by the state, such as property records, marriage licenses, and birth and death certificates. The county clerk performs election duties and can be appointed to issue state hunting and fishing licenses. These are just a few examples of the way the county acts as an arm of state government.

However, one of the counties' largest tasks is administering various health and human services programs, particularly Medicaid, a federal-state health insurance program for low-income and disabled residents. In 2010, the number of participants in Medicaid was equal to about 20% of the state population.

As a unit of local self-government, the county is given powers by the state to handle local matters. However, its administrative power is limited by the Wisconsin Constitution and state statutes. For example, a county cannot abolish or consolidate an office that is required by the constitution. Thus, counties do not have the broad home-rule that largely allows cities and villages to decide how to manage their own affairs (see Chapter 7).

The county may build parks, maintain county forests, take care of county highways, provide mental health services, and operate county homes for the aged and physically disabled. While it may provide only those services that are required or permitted, it does have some control over how its government is organized and administered.

Organization of County Government

Counties can vary slightly in how their government is organized, but they all have the same basic structure.

County Board of Supervisors

County Board of Supervisors
The legislative branch of county government. In some cases, it may also function as the executive branch.

The **county board of supervisors** passes ordinances (laws) and resolutions. Most boards divide into committees to handle their duties. Some examples of board committees are finance, personnel, human services, law enforcement, highways, parks, and zoning. A committee considers problems that arise in its area of authority. Sometimes it does this by recommending that the board, as a whole, take necessary action. The board usually follows a committee's recommendations.

In counties without an executive or administrator, the committee also supervises departments assigned to it. For example, the highway committee supervises the county highway department.

Each supervisor on the county board is elected from a supervisory district. The county's population should be divided about equally among the districts. If necessary, following the federal population census conducted every 10 years, the county board must redraw the districts to be sure they are approximately equal in population.

All supervisors are elected on a nonpartisan basis for two-year terms, except in Milwaukee County, where the term is four years. The maximum number of county supervisors is limited by state law depending on the county's population, as indicated in the table below. The board may have fewer members if it chooses or if the county voters pass a referendum.

Two counties, Milwaukee and Menominee, have county boards based on a different system of representation. The size of the Milwaukee County board is determined by the board.

In Menominee County, which has only one town, the entire town board also serves as the county board of supervisors. Thus, the Menominee County board has seven members.

County boards are required by law to meet at least twice a year. The April meeting is an organizational meeting in which the board elects its officers and names its committees. The purpose of the fall meeting in October or November is to adopt the annual county budget. Other meetings are held as often as necessary. Many county boards meet at least monthly.

County Executive
The most powerful of county officers. They are elected to a four-year term and are independent of the county board.

County Administration

As county duties and services became more complex, state law was changed to permit selection of a single officer to manage county government. If elected, this official is called a **county executive**. Elected to a four-year term, they are the most powerful of county officers and are independent of the county board. If appointed by the county board, the title is **county administrator,** or administrative coordinator.

County Administrator
The administrative head of county government appointed by the county board.

Table 6.2

Number of County Board Supervisors (2012)

Population Group	No. of Counties	Max. No. of Supervisors	Range of Supervisors
100,000-499,999	14	47	11-38
50,000-99,999	13	39	15-33
25,000-49,999	18	31	17-31
Less than 25,000	25	21	11-21

Note: Milwaukee and Menominee are not included because they are treated separately by state law.

A 1962 constitutional amendment authorizing an elected county executive in Milwaukee County was the first step toward this type of county government administration. Under state law, Milwaukee County must have an executive. A later constitutional amendment, ratified in 1969, allows all Wisconsin counties to create the position of executive or administrator if they choose.

In many respects, the duties of the two positions are similar. Both the executive and administrator manage the affairs of the county, submit an annual budget, and make certain appointments to office. There are some differences, however. A county executive is elected on a nonpartisan ballot by the people for a four-year term and is independent of the county board. The executive has the power to veto county board actions, including a partial veto on appropriations. On the other hand, a county administrator is selected by the county board to serve at its pleasure for an indefinite term and has no veto power.

As of June 2011, 12 counties had county executives and 24 had county administrators. One county had both a county executive and county administrator. State law requires counties without an executive or administrator to appoint an administrative coordinator who is responsible for management functions not vested in other local officials.

As demands on counties became more complex, populous counties often turned to either an elected executive or appointed administrator to help manage county government. In fact, as of 2011, the 10 most populous counties had either a county executive (seven), a county administrator (two), or both (one).

Other County Officials

Each county is required by the state constitution or state law to elect certain officials whose duties are set forth by state law. These are a district attorney, sheriff, clerk, treasurer, register of deeds, clerk of circuit court, coroner (unless the county has a medical examiner system), and surveyor (unless that officer is appointed). Milwaukee County does not elect a coroner or a surveyor. Although the district attorney is elected by county voters, it is designated a state office and the state pays the salary.

In contrast to county supervisors, these county officials are elected on a partisan basis. They run in the November general election and receive party support for their campaigns. A constitutional amendment adopted in 2005 changed the term of office for these officials from two to four years.

The **county clerk** manages elections for county offices, administers various licenses, and serves as secretary to the county board. In counties without an executive or administrator, the clerk may compile budget requests for the board to review and keep financial records on income and expenditures.

County Clerk
Manages elections for county offices, administers various licenses, and serves as secretary to the county board.

Another elected official, the **county treasurer**, handles all county government funds. The treasurer must receive and record all revenues coming into the county treasury and ensure that the money is paid out as required by the budget.

County Treasurer
Handles all county government funds.

Several criticisms have been raised about the organization of county government. Some say that the county board should be concerned with lawmaking and not be burdened with administrative details. They would like to see wider use of

Counties operate and maintain about 20,000 miles of county highways.

an executive or administrator with broad powers to handle day-to-day county matters. Others have complained that having so many independently elected county officers splits responsibility. County board size has been hotly debated in some counties in recent years.

6.2 COUNTY ACTIVITIES AND FINANCING

Your county does many things, both as a unit of local government and as an agent of the state. Figure 6.2 below shows how much is spent on major county services.

Health and Human Services

Generally, health and human services is the most significant area in county government, averaging 40% of a county's budget.

The county also provides special services to disabled or elderly persons and certifies medical assistance and food stamp benefits. Some counties operate a nursing home. Others provide general health and mental health programs.

Most health-related expenditures are paid by federal and state governments on behalf of patients served. The payments can

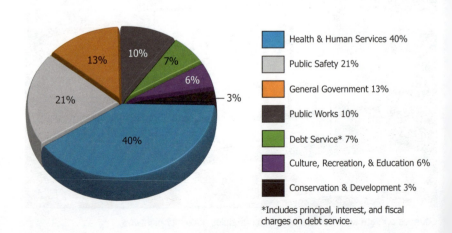

Figure 6.2
County Expenditure Dollar (2011)

Health & Human Services 40%
Public Safety 21%
General Government 13%
Public Works 10%
Debt Service* 7%
Culture, Recreation, & Education 6%
Conservation & Development 3%

*Includes principal, interest, and fiscal charges on debt service.

be for less than the actual cost, prompting criticism from local government officials of **unfunded mandates** from state and federal governments.

Highways

The county has always been important for highway transportation. Each county has a highway department directed by a highway commissioner with oversight from the county board's highway committee. Counties operate and maintain about 20,000 miles of county highways.

Counties also handle snow removal, salting, and upkeep on state and interstate highways. This work is performed under contract with the state. Counties may also construct and maintain roads for cities, villages, and towns, if asked. Cities, villages, and towns reimburse counties for this work.

Public Safety

The sheriff is a county's chief police officer. The sheriff and his deputies arrest persons accused of committing crimes and run the county jail. In most counties, the sheriff enforces the traffic laws. In a few counties, there is a separate county traffic patrol that enforces traffic laws.

Unfunded Mandates
Programs or rules imposed by the state or federal government without adequate funding to pay for their implementation.

Figure 6.3

County Income Dollar (2011)

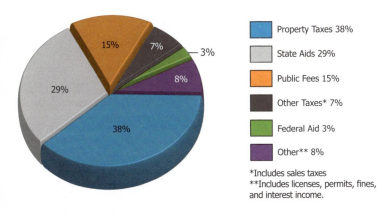

Property Taxes 38%
State Aids 29%
Public Fees 15%
Other Taxes* 7%
Federal Aid 3%
Other** 8%

*Includes sales taxes
**Includes licenses, permits, fines, and interest income.

> ### County Sales Tax in Wisconsin
>
> In 1969, the state legislature gave counties the authority to enact a 0.5% sales tax. The tax is "piggybacked" on the state sales tax. It applies to the same items and services taxed by the state.
>
> Between 1969 and 1985, no counties adopted a sales tax because they could not keep the tax collections. The money had to be distributed among the cities, villages, and towns in the county. In 1985, state law was changed to allow counties to keep the tax proceeds. Today, 62 of Wisconsin's 72 counties have adopted a 0.5% sales tax.
>
> State law says the county sales tax must be used for "property tax relief." However, research shows this may not be the case in many counties.

District Attorney
An official elected by county voters who acts as prosecutor for the state.

Another important law enforcement official in the county is the **district attorney.** This official represents the government when a criminal case goes to court. The district attorney is elected locally but paid by the state.

If a death appears to be due to unnatural causes, the county coroner may be called to investigate whether a crime has occurred. Instead of a coroner, Milwaukee County employs a physician as a medical examiner. Other counties may replace the coroner with a medical examiner system if they wish.

County Sales Tax
A 0.5% optional tax collected on retail sales that funds county services.

Financing County Government

Figure 6.3 on page 83 shows the major county revenues. They are charges for public services (such as nursing home fees), state and federal aids (especially for social services, mental health, and highways), the **county sales tax,** and the county property tax.

REVIEW

Wisconsin's 72 counties have dual roles; they act as arms of the state, but also serve as local units of government. While counties provide many services, their focus is on health and human service programs (primarily Medicaid) and corrections (county jails). County boards range in size, and members generally serve two-year terms. County heads vary from powerful county executives to part-time administrative coordinators. ◻

Key Terms in This Chapter

- Counties
- County Board of Supervisors
- County Executive
- County Administrator
- County Clerk
- County Treasurer
- Unfunded Mandates
- District Attorney
- County Sales Tax

7 Cities & Villages

Wisconsin has three types of municipal governments: cities, villages, and towns. About 70% of the state's population lives in either a city or village. These two types of municipality have many similarities, but also differ in important ways.

IN THIS CHAPTER:

- 7.1 What Are Cities and Villages? (87)
- 7.2 How Cities and Villages Are Created (87)
- 7.3 City and Village Finances (93)
- 7.4 Putting Property Taxes in Perspective (99)

7.1 WHAT ARE CITIES AND VILLAGES?

Cities and villages are granted broad authority under the Wisconsin Constitution to govern themselves without state interference. They are run by councils or boards elected to represent voters' wishes and to handle government business on their behalf. This is called **representative government**.

A city or village is created from an area originally in a town. The new unit of government is called a municipal corporation. Another way of describing this is to say the village or city is incorporated.

A town does not have much independence in the action it can take. It is more like a subdivision of the state that provides local government services. Though town residents can vote at town meetings (direct democracy), the structure of the town, its officials, and some services are set by the state. By contrast, cities and villages are much more independent.

Representative Government
A form of democracy in which elected people represent the larger citizenry.

7.2 HOW CITIES AND VILLAGES ARE CREATED

Why do people decide to organize as a village or city with its own governing body? There are many reasons. One is that people living close together frequently want to have sidewalks, street lights, full-time police and fire protection, or other services. Other town residents who do not need such services may not want to pay for them. One solution would be to form a city or village that can provide the desired services.

All or part of a town may **incorporate** as a village or city if it follows certain procedures. First, the people who wish to incorporate must get a specific number of supporting signatures from persons who are both voters and property owners in the area. Then, the plan must be approved by the circuit court and the Wisconsin Department of Administration (DOA). Finally, the residents of the area vote on whether to incorporate. (The people in the part of the town that will not be affected by the change do not vote.) A majority of those who vote on the question must approve the incorporation in order for it to take effect.

Incorporate
Merge into one united governmental unit.

The state of Wisconsin sets high standards for establishing new cities and villages. In 2003, Wisconsin Act 171 established a five-member Incorporation Review Board to review petitions of territories seeking to incorporate as a city or village and to determine if the petition meets certain public-interest standards. Examples of recent incorporations include the villages of Summit (Waukesha County) in 2010; Caledonia (Racine County) in 2005; Bellevue, Hobart, and Suamico (Brown County) and Lake Hallie (Chippewa County) in 2003; and Kronenwetter (Marathon County) in 2002.

Boundary Changes

Annexation
The process by which part of an adjoining town is added to a city or village.

Once incorporated, cities and villages may grow in area by a procedure called **annexation**. Annexation involves taking a part of an adjoining town and adding it to the city or village. Property owners in the town usually initiate the process by filing an annexation petition with the municipality. Approval by the city council or village board and voters is required. In some cases, an advisory review by the DOA is also necessary. Generally, after these steps are completed, the area transfers to the city or village. The area's residents become city or village residents and they vote and pay taxes in their new jurisdiction.

Consolidation
The process by which two or more adjoining units of government merge into one unit.

A city, village, or town may also grow by **consolidation**. With this process, two or more separate units of government located next to each other vote to merge into one unit. This requires a two-thirds vote from each governing body and approval of a majority of the residents of each unit involved. The merger may occur between towns, villages, cities, or any combination of municipalities. A consolidation involving a town must be approved by a circuit court and the DOA.

Incorporation, annexation, and consolidation are complicated, and there are detailed state laws that must be followed in each case.

Population Differences

In 2011, there were 190 cities and 405 villages in the state. Cities often have more people than villages. Most Wisconsin villages have fewer than 1,000 residents. The smallest, Big Falls, has a population of 79. Some villages are exceptionally large. The largest is Menomonee Falls with over 35,000 people. When a village's population reaches 1,000, it can choose to become a city, but it does not have to change. The largest city in the state is Milwaukee, with a population of about 595,000. Madison is second, with a population of about 233,000. Thirteen other cities in Wisconsin have populations over 40,000. The eight smallest cities each have a population under 1,000. The smallest, Bayfield, has about 500 residents.

Organizational Differences

Although the broad powers of villages and cities are similar, their governments are organized differently.

A village is governed by a **board of trustees** that is generally elected at-large. This means the trustees are chosen from the village as a whole rather than from smaller districts. Ordinarily, a village with a population of 350 or less elects two trustees, while larger villages elect six. Trustees are elected for two-year terms in spring nonpartisan elections.

Board of Trustees
The governing body of a village elected at large.

People also elect their village president. Like any other board member, the president votes on matters before the board but has no authority to veto board actions.

Other elected village officers may include a clerk, treasurer, assessor, constable, or municipal judge.

The governing body for cities is the **common council**. Council members are usually called **alderpersons**. They are elected on a nonpartisan basis and, in most cases, serve two-year terms. In some cities, alderpersons are elected at-large. In most, the city is divided into aldermanic districts, and citizens vote only for the aldermanic candidates running in the district where they live. Some cities have a combination of at-large and district seats. Most large cities subdivide the districts into smaller sections called wards, but all wards within a particular district vote for the same list of aldermanic candidates.

Common Council
The elected governing body of a city.

The number of aldermanic districts may vary among cities, but boundary lines are supposed to be drawn so there is an approximately equal number of residents in each of the city's districts.

Alderpersons
Elected members of the common council.

The chief executive officer in most cities is the **mayor**, who is usually elected for a two-year term. Most large cities in Wisconsin have a four-year term for mayor, while others provide for a three-year term. Some cities have term limits

> **Mayor**
> The title of a city's chief elected executive officer.

for how long a mayor can serve. The mayor is a member of the common council, presides at council meetings, and has authority to vote only in case of a tie. The mayor may veto council actions. The council may override (cancel) the veto if two-thirds of the council votes to do so. In all except the largest cities, the mayor is usually a part-time official.

Various officials, including a clerk, treasurer, assessor, engineer, and attorney, help the mayor run the city. They may be elected by the people, appointed by the council, or appointed by the mayor. In most cases, the mayor's appointments must be approved by the council.

City and Village Home Rule

Cities and villages have special challenges in providing services. Streets must be built to withstand heavy traffic. Sidewalks and streets must be well lit and properly drained. Underground networks of pipelines must be built to supply large numbers of people with water and sewer services. Solid waste must be collected and properly discarded. Crime must be controlled and fire protection must be provided.

> **Home Rule**
> Allows cities and villages to decide how to manage their own affairs, unless the state constitution prohibits it.

City and village governments have been given wide-ranging powers to deal with these problems. A 1924 constitutional amendment granted them broad authority, known as **home rule**. This means that a city or village may do things the way it wants unless the state constitution does not allow it, or the activity is something of statewide concern that the legislature should handle. Within these limits, the governing bodies of the cities and villages may adopt their own laws, called **ordinances**.

> **Ordinances**
> Legislation enacted by a municipal unit of government.

A city or village operates under a general **charter**, comparable to a state constitution. The charter is a set of rules outlining the way each unit has decided to organize and carry out its duties. Long ago, the state legislature passed laws granting a special charter to each city and village as it was incorporated. The state enacted a general charter law for villages in 1871 and a similar law for cities in 1892. Today, the local unit may adopt its own charter within provisions set by state law. The charter can be changed by a charter ordinance, which may be subject to voter approval.

Figure 7.1
Types of City Government

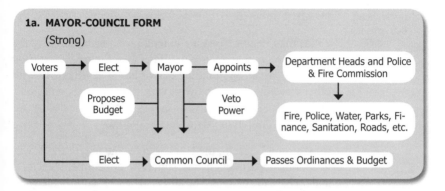

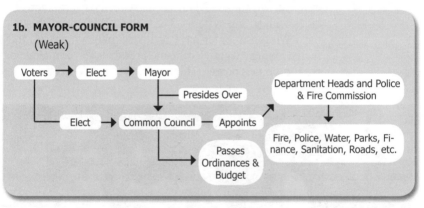

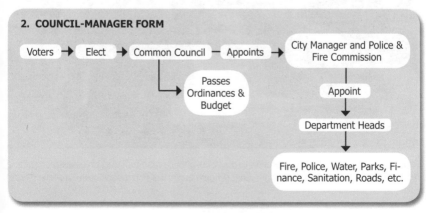

Charter
A set of rules outlining the way a unit of municipal government performs its duties.

Home rule allows cities and villages to organize to meet their own needs. By passing a charter ordinance, they may determine whether certain officials will be appointed or elected and the length of their terms, as well as whether some offices may be combined.

Cities may decide, to some extent, how much authority the mayor should have over city affairs (see Figure 7.1 on page 91). In a "weak" system, the mayor has to share power with other elected officers and with various boards, commissions, and independent officials. In this system, responsibility for the administration of city affairs is shared.

In a "strong" system, the council gives the mayor the power to appoint department heads, supervise government services, and prepare the budget. The aim is to be well-coordinated and efficient. Milwaukee, Madison, and Green Bay are among the cities with strong systems. Throughout Wisconsin's history, most Wisconsin cities have had weak mayors because they feared giving executive officers (president, governor, mayor, etc.) too much power. The current trend in Wisconsin is to give mayors more power.

The Port Washington city engineer talks to residents about a road construction assessment after a Port Washington Common Council meeting. (Photo courtesy of Port Washington-Saukville Patch.)

Many cities and villages have created the position of **administrator** to strengthen municipal management. The administrator's duties may range from serving as an executive assistant to handling budgeting, purchasing, and personnel, as well as supervising public works, parks, and police and fire services. The administrator's authority depends on the wishes of the village board or the mayor and common council. About 80 cities and about 83 villages employ an administrator in a full-time or combined position.

Administrator
A person hired to strengthen the management of a city or village.

Another form of government that cities and villages can choose under home rule is the council-manager form. In this system, the council or board is usually small and elected on an at-large basis. It hires a professionally trained manager, who serves at its pleasure for an indefinite term, to carry out its directions and see that government services are delivered as planned.

The manager form of government is based on the idea that there should be a separation between the voters' representatives, who decide what government should do and an administrator, who sees that it gets done. Managers do not preside over council or board meetings and have no veto power. They may appoint their department heads and have responsibility for budget preparation. There are about 20 city managers and 11 village managers in Wisconsin. Cities with managers include Janesville, Fond du Lac, and Eau Claire. Brown Deer and Whitefish Bay are examples of villages with managers.

7.3 CITY AND VILLAGE FINANCES

Cities and villages provide many services to their citizens. Some of these municipalities, particularly the smallest, limit their activities to essential services, such as providing for streets, water and sewer systems, and solid waste collection. They may maintain a small police force and a volunteer fire department. As a general rule, when cities and villages grow in size, more services are needed, including libraries, parks, and recreational facilities. But, all these services cost money. The type and quality of service provided will depend on how much people are willing to pay.

The cost of new public buildings, streets, sewers, or parks may be too expensive to pay all at once. The council or board may decide to spread the cost of a project over 20 or more years. It does this by borrowing money and paying some back each year, along with interest.

If it borrows, a village or city must impose an annual property tax that cannot be repealed until the loan is repaid. State law limits the amount a municipality can borrow. In some cases, before a local unit may borrow money, voters must approve the loan.

The Budget

Perhaps the most important job of a common council or a village board is to decide how money is to be used during the year. How much should be spent? For what purposes? How high should taxes be? These questions are answered when a city or village budget is discussed and approved each year.

The city or village budget outlines the services to be provided and their projected cost for the coming year. It also shows how much income is expected during the year.

In developing the expenditure (spending) portion of the budget, many questions have to be answered. Some examples are: Should the city buy a new fire truck? How many employees

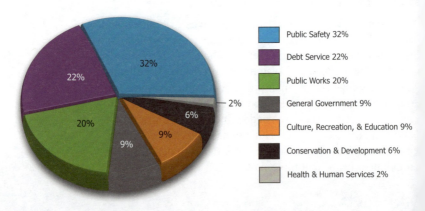

Figure 7.2

City Expenditure Dollar (2011)

- Public Safety 32%
- Debt Service 22%
- Public Works 20%
- General Government 9%
- Culture, Recreation, & Education 9%
- Conservation & Development 6%
- Health & Human Services 2%

are needed to handle the government's services? Should the city develop a new park?

In developing the revenue part of the budget, elected officials have to determine how much tax revenue is needed and whether there are opportunities to obtain funding through user fees, naming rights, donations, or other means. In Wisconsin, cities and villages are limited by state law as to how much they can increase property taxes.

The budget process should interest all citizens. This is their chance to tell their representatives what they want government to do and how much they are willing to pay. State law requires that a public hearing be held on the budget before it is adopted. The place and time of the hearing must be publicized in advance. Any resident or taxpayer who attends the hearing is entitled by the state's open meetings law to provide comment on the budget. However, the law does not guarantee you can speak. Rather, it guarantees a forum where you can have input. The presiding officer still gets to limit or control the amount of time people can speak and the length of the hearing. Often, people are invited to register on paper and leave written comments.

Figures 7.2 on page 94 and 7.3 below show how a typical city or village spends its dollars on services. The services they provide are similar. Remember, however, that the total

Figure 7.3

Village Expenditure Dollar (2011)

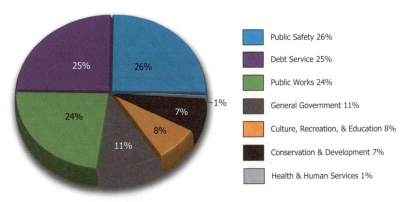

Property Taxes
A tax on property levied by municipalities based on the estimated value of property.

actual dollar amount spent may be quite different, depending on the population of the city or village and the amount of service provided.

The Property Tax

When a city or village knows what it wants to do and how much it will cost, those planning the budget must figure out how the money will be raised to meet these expenses. First, they estimate the income expected from sources such as fees, federal and state aids, and other small revenue sources. This amount is then subtracted from the costs. The remaining cost is financed by **property taxes**. The total amount of money to be raised through these taxes is called the **property tax levy**.

Property Tax Levy
The amount of money raised through the property tax to finance local government services.

As the example on the next page shows, if a city needed $1,000,000 to finance its annual operations, and $600,000 could be raised from federal aids, state aids, and other revenues, the remaining $400,000 would be financed with the property tax levy. However, state-imposed limits on property taxes may mean the city or village has to cut costs to stay within the limits.

In other words, the property tax levy is the revenue source of last resort. It is used to balance local revenues and expenditures.

Figure 7.4

City Income Dollar (2011)

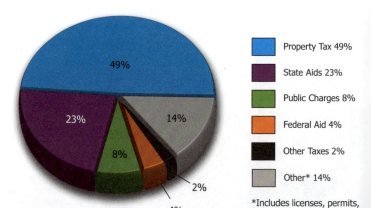

Property Tax 49%
State Aids 23%
Public Charges 8%
Federal Aid 4%
Other Taxes 2%
Other* 14%

*Includes licenses, permits, fines, and interest earnings.

Chapter Seven 97

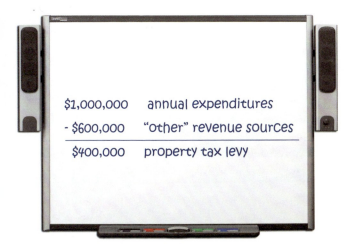

Figures 7.4 on page 96 and 7.5 below show that general property taxes are the largest source of city and village income. They are also used by town and county governments, as well as schools. Property taxes are paid by owners of land, homes, farms, businesses, and factories. The property taxes that are levied by the various local units of government are collected by the town, village, or city in which the property is located. A property owner receives only one **property tax bill** each

Property Tax Bill
The amount charged to each property owner by taxing authorities.

Figure 7.5

Village Income Dollar (2011)

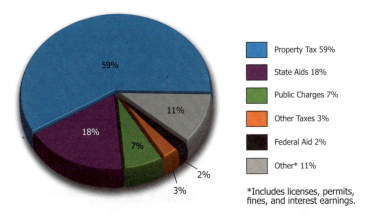

*Includes licenses, permits, fines, and interest earnings.

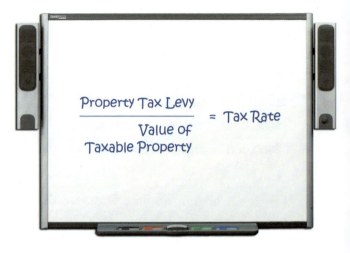

year. The bill lists the amount charged by each taxing authority (municipality, county, public school district, technical college, etc.). After the money is collected, it is distributed to the various taxing units according to the amount each unit levied.

Property Tax Rate
The property tax levy divided by the total value of property in a taxing unit.

The **property tax rate** is the total amount of property taxes to be collected by a local unit of government (property tax levy) divided by the total value of taxable property in that taxing district.

Assume that a city needs to levy $400,000 in property taxes and all taxable property in the city is valued at $40,000,000.

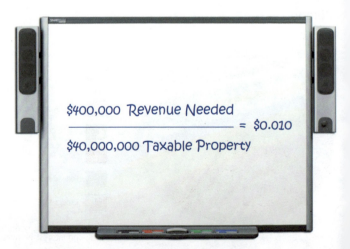

The amount to be raised ($400,000) would be divided by the value of the taxable property ($40,000,000). The result would be a property tax rate of $0.010 for each dollar of taxable property.

This tax rate is usually expressed as $10 per $1,000 of property valuation. Thus, a taxpayer with a home valued at $120,000 would owe $10 × $120, or $1,200, in property taxes.

7.4 PUTTING PROPERTY TAXES IN PERSPECTIVE

Wisconsin Rapids is an "average" sized Wisconsin city. The 2013 budget to operate the City of Wisconsin Rapids was $25,083,840.

To help fund this amount, the city taxes home owners $12.22 per $1,000 of value of their home. Thus, a person owning a home valued at $100,000 would pay $1,220 for the city portion of their property tax bill ($12.22 × $100,000 in value). What does the taxpayer get for her money? She gets 131 employees including:

- A full time mayor, city attorney, clerk, and treasurer;
- A full time police department staffed by 36 officers;
- A full time fire department staffed by 32 officers;
- An elected common council;
- Joint ownership of a municipal airport;
- Streets, lighting, sewer and water service;
- Snow plowing;
- Garbage and recycling pick-up;
- A senior center;
- A public library;
- Eight parks, two athletic fields, one zoo, and one pool.

How Much Is $25 Million?

Entertainer Lady Gaga made $25,353,039 in 2011, ranking number four in Billboard Magazine's 2012 Music Money Makers list. In the lead was Taylor Swift, pulling in $35.7 million.

REVIEW

Cities and villages share many of the same powers and perform many of the same services for their residents. Both may change their organization and operations to fit their local needs due to the home rule provisions in the state constitution and state law. ☐

Key Terms in This Chapter

- Representative Government
- Incorporate
- Annexation
- Consolidation
- Board of Trustees
- Common Council
- Alderpersons
- Mayor
- Home Rule
- Ordinances
- Charter
- Administrator
- Property Taxes
- Property Tax Levy
- Property Tax Bill
- Property Tax Rate

8 Towns

Towns date back to the early days of colonial America. They are the form of government closest to a "direct democracy," a system in which every person takes a direct part. Attendance at town meetings depends on voter interest, but those who attend decide how the town will operate. All qualified residents (age 18 or over, who have lived in the town for at least 10 days) can vote on town matters at the annual meeting. They even get to discuss and vote on their own municipal property tax levy each year.

IN THIS CHAPTER:

- 8.1 What is a Town? (103)
- 8.2 Powers of the Town (107)

8.1 WHAT IS A TOWN?

The **town** form of government was brought to Wisconsin by early settlers from New York and New England. It was first authorized in 1827, when present-day Wisconsin was part of the Michigan Territory. Wisconsin towns developed as subdivisions of the state and county government to deliver local services in rural areas.

Town
Unit of local government that serves primarily rural areas.

Today, the town continues to play an important part in providing services, particularly to rural areas. Any area in Wisconsin that is not in a city or village is part of a town. Whenever the word "town" is used in this book, it refers to a unit of local government. There is some confusion about the term. For example, people might refer to their "hometown" but really mean a village or small city. However, as the term is used here, we are referring to a distinct unit of local government that exists to provide services to its residents. Its proper name is town, not township. Township is a surveyor's term that describes a basic grid for legal descriptions of land.

Towns serve 1.7 million residents, or 30.1% of the state's population. The 1,257 towns in Wisconsin vary widely in size. The largest, Menominee, contains 230,000 acres (357.96 square miles) and covers all of Menominee County. Some of

The state-operated Merrimac Ferry shuttles traffic across the Wisconsin River between the Towns of West Point and Merrimac. (Photo by Mark Anderson, courtesy of Merrimac Communications.)

the smallest towns contain only a few thousand acres. The Town of Germantown in Washington County is the smallest town in the state at 1.7 square miles. The populations of towns also vary from fewer than 50 residents to over 23,000. More than 1,000 towns have populations under 2,000; only 59 exceed 4,000.

Town residents depend on town government to provide certain basic services like road maintenance. Towns hold elections, collect taxes, and maintain order. The size and density of the population determines, to some extent, what other kinds of services are needed by the people living in a town. For example, rural towns composed of farms are generally not called on to provide street lights, sidewalks, garbage col-

One Town's Story

The Town of York in Green County was settled by immigrants from Norway and Switzerland. The terrain reminded them of their homelands.

In 1838, John Stewart settled in the area now called Postville, formerly named Stewart. Other settlers were William C. Green, Amos Conkey, Albert Green, Albro and William Crowel, and Ezra Wescott.

Two Norwegian Lutheran churches were established in the Town of York. York Memorial Church is the only active church in the town today.

A sawmill operated in the mid-1800s on the east bank of Sawmill Creek. It provided lumber for farms and homesteads. By 1890, no record of the mill remained.

Cheese factories were vital to the life of all residents. Fourteen factories were humming at one time. There were at least three post offices in the town at the turn of the 20th century. Mail came from Mineral Point through the Town of Moscow, and then to York by stagecoach.

About that time, there were 200 farms raising cows, pigs, chickens, sheep, and horses. Some also grew wheat, oats, barley, corn, and soybeans. Now there are about 32 farms, most raising heifers and steers, and a few raising sheep or goats.

The owners of today's farms often work off the farm, many commuting to nearby cities for jobs.

Cross country skiers at the Minocqua Winter Park in the Town of Minocqua. (Photo courtesy of Mike Cozzi.)

lection, or water and sewerage systems. However, people in more populated towns might want these and other services.

Service Problems

Special problems might arise if the population is concentrated in one part of the town. People living on farms and those living in built-up areas might disagree about what services are needed, and rural residents might object to paying for services they do not want.

One way to settle questions of what services the town should offer, and who should pay the costs, is by setting the boundaries of the built-up area and calling it a **utility district**. This area is not a separate government unit. It is still part of the town in which it is located. But, the additional services are provided only inside the boundaries of the utility district, and the owners of the property within that district are the only ones taxed to pay for them.

Scattered throughout most of rural Wisconsin are small built-up areas identified as unincorporated villages. This term is

Utility District
A more developed area of a town that provides additional services to citizens and levies additional taxes to provide them.

used solely for identification purposes. These areas are still part of a town. An unincorporated village may or may not be a utility district.

Urban Towns

Town Meeting
Annual meeting of qualified voters to decide important town issues. An example of "direct democracy."

A town or part of a town in a heavily populated area often looks like a city or village. Houses are close together, often with stores and shopping centers nearby. The town's residents who live in this urbanized area might lead quite different lives from those in the more rural parts of the town. They might decide to break off from the town by establishing their own separate city or village government or by attaching their area to an existing city or village.

If areas break away, the town becomes smaller. It might even cease to exist if it is combined with another government unit. For example, Milwaukee County originally had seven towns, but now all town area is included in a city or village and the county contains no town governments. In some cases, urban towns continue to thrive, however, by offering services similar to those a city or village would provide.

Town Meeting and Town Board Powers

Annual Town Meeting (held by state law on the third Tuesday in April or within 10 days after)
- Levies taxes for town operation or delegates the authority to the town board.
- Authorizes the town board to buy or sell town property.
- Sets the salaries of town officers.
- Authorizes the town board to issue general obligation bonds.
- Authorizes the town board to exercise "village powers."

Town Board of Supervisors (ranging from three to seven by state law)
- Oversees all town affairs, except those duties delegated by state law to other town officers or employees.
- Adopts the town budget, after a public hearing.
- Provides law enforcement, fire protection, and ambulance services.
- Manages any legal action to which the town is a party.
- Levies town taxes if authorized by the annual town meeting.

8.2 POWERS OF THE TOWN

State law allows cities and villages more choice than towns regarding how they organize and what services they provide. For example, cities and villages are free to decide which officials and department heads they will use to run their governments, but town officials are set by state law. Town boards may be authorized at the town meeting to use some of the powers of villages to provide services and regulate certain activities.

Town Meeting

Some decisions on town operations are made by direct action of the qualified voters who gather at the town hall for the annual **town meeting**. Voters attending this meeting determine what the town will do, within the limits of state law. Usual business includes setting the salaries of elected town officers and determining the amount of town taxes for the coming year. Questions about town services may also be discussed. Sometimes, special meetings are held in addition to the annual meeting. The town meeting is one of the few remaining examples of **direct democracy**.

Brule Town Hall in northwestern Wisconsin is the site of town board meetings on the second Tuesday of each month. The April meeting is the annual meeting.

Given the voters' ability to vote directly on major town issues, you would expect town meetings to be popular, well-attended events. However, most town meetings draw few people, unless a controversial issue generates interest. Another challenge with the town meeting is that, in populous towns, large gatherings of voters make it difficult to debate issues and find consensus on decisions.

The Town of Brule is named for the Brule River, known as the "River of Presidents." Grant, Coolidge (pictured above, left), Cleveland, Hoover (above, right), and Eisenhower came to fish for trout, steelhead, and salmon. They stayed at Cedar Island Lodge, and Coolidge kept a summer office in Superior. (Photo courtesy of Douglas County Historical Society.)

Direct Democracy
Every eligible voter (as opposed to only elected officials) has the right to vote on decisions before the legislative body.

Town Supervisors
Elected officials charged with running the town.

Town Chair
A town supervisor elected to preside at town meetings and board meetings.

The day-to-day job of running the town is handled by the town board, which usually is made up of three **town supervisors**, one of whom is elected **town chair**. The supervisors are elected in odd-numbered years at the spring election. They hold office for two-year terms. Supervisors are part-time officers unless designated as full-time by the town meeting.

A town board authorized to exercise village powers may increase the number of supervisors to four or five. These supervisors are elected to staggered two-year terms. The Town of Menominee is allowed seven board members.

According to law, there are certain things only a town meeting can authorize. Other things the town board can handle on its own. The list on page 106 shows some of the powers of the town meeting and the town board.

Other elected town officials include a town clerk, a treasurer, an assessor (unless chosen by appointment or through a civil service system), and in some cases, a constable who helps keep the peace. In nearly all cases, town officials are only part-time. Their duties are set by law.

The **town clerk** acts as secretary for the town meeting and the town board, records all official proceedings, and has charge of the town's official records. This officer keeps records of

Figure 8.1

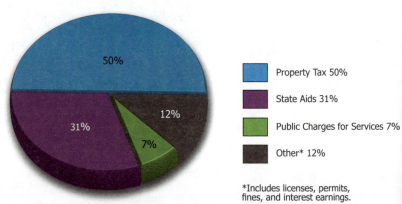

Town Income Dollar (2011)

- Property Tax 50%
- State Aids 31%
- Public Charges for Services 7%
- Other* 12%

*Includes licenses, permits, fines, and interest earnings.

the town's finances and supervises all elections held in the town. The **town treasurer** has charge of all money belonging to the town. This involves paying the town's bills and collecting taxes and other revenues (money received by the town).

The **assessor** makes a list of all taxable property in the town and determines how much each parcel of property is worth, except manufacturing property, which is assessed by the Wisconsin Department of Revenue.

In most towns, law enforcement is handled by the county sheriff. In some, a town constable enforces the law.

Town Finances

Figures 8.1 on page 108 and 8.2 below show how a typical town receives and spends its money. About 30% of a typical town's income comes from the state in shared revenues and other state aids.

About 50% of its revenue, on average, is raised through local property taxes paid by landowners.

A town's main activity is usually building and maintaining local roads. Much of the state aid given to towns is for this purpose. Towns maintain 62,038 miles of town highways—approximately half of the 112,362 miles of public highways

Town Clerk
Official who keeps all of the town's records.

Town Treasurer
Official in charge of the town's money.

Assessor
Official charged with determining the value of property for taxation purposes.

Figure 8.2

Town Expenditure Dollar (2011)

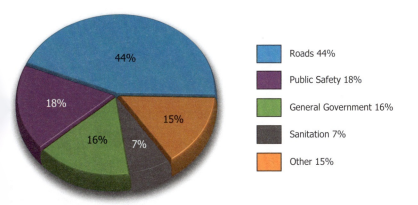

in Wisconsin. A typical town uses about half of its money for roads and other public works. Some town boards contract with county government for road work.

A town spends money on other items that are usually less costly. Sometimes, the town contracts with a nearby city or village for fire protection. Some towns have organized volunteer fire departments.

REVIEW

Wisconsin is one of more than 20 states in the nation that use town government to provide local services to people living outside cities or villages. More than 30% of Wisconsin's citizens live in towns. Individual towns vary widely in terms of population and property value, but all are organized according to state law. Most towns provide only minimal services, such as snow plowing, road repair, and fire protection. Some are more like city and village governments and provide police protection, parks, and solid waste collection. ☐

Key Terms in This Chapter

- Town
- Utility District
- Town Meeting
- Direct Democracy
- Town Supervisors
- Town Chair
- Town Clerk
- Town Treasurer
- Assessor

9 Education

Public education touches the lives of many people—not only pupils in school, but also parents, teachers, and the taxpayers who pay for schools. It is the single most expensive service that state and local governments provide. Many Wisconsin students benefit from tax-supported schooling from the day they begin school until they complete high school, technical college, or university training.

IN THIS CHAPTER:

- 9.1 School Districts (113)
- 9.2 Financing Schools (116)
- 9.3 Alternatives to Public Schools (117)
- 9.4 Wisconsin Technical College System (118)
- 9.5 University of Wisconsin System (120)

9.1 SCHOOL DISTRICTS

Wisconsin's constitution requires the legislature to create district schools throughout the state to provide free public elementary and secondary education to all children. This education is supported by an annual school tax levied by each district. For the 2012 school year, total costs averaged $12,012 for each student attending public elementary or secondary school in Wisconsin.

State Supervision

The state constitution directs the state superintendent of public instruction to supervise public schools. The nonpartisan superintendent is elected in the spring to a four-year term.

While actual operation of public elementary and secondary schools is left mainly to local school authorities, the state is responsible for enforcing certain minimum standards. One of those standards requires school districts to schedule at least 180 school days each year. To carry out this responsibility, state school officials consult with local school district boards and administrators.

The state also provides money to operate most local schools. The funds the state distributes are called **school aids**. These include general aids and special (categorical) aids. General aids help pay instructional and other operating costs. Special aids support transportation, special education, and other specific programs. One way the state can enforce its minimum standards is by withholding a portion of a district's state aids if its requirements are not met.

School Aids
Financial support that state government distributes to local school districts for the operation of local schools.

In general, state school aids are distributed to promote three objectives: (1) to provide reasonably equal educational opportunities for all students, (2) to encourage local districts to improve their educational programs, and (3) to keep the property tax rates as equitable as possible.

The state also has set up regional organizations to help provide certain school services more efficiently and cost-effectively within each part of the state. There are 12 such organizations, called Cooperative Educational Service Agencies (**CESA**). These receive no direct tax dollars. Instead, they sell services to individual school districts, which choose to contract for

CESA
Agency created by the legislature to coordinate regional educational services.

special services they might not otherwise be able to afford, such as school psychologists, occupational therapists, or professional development for teachers. Cooperative purchasing of items such as supplies or services through a CESA allows smaller districts to obtain a better price when buying.

The governing board of each CESA (called the board of control) is composed of representatives from the area's school boards. The board appoints an administrator to handle a CESA's day-to-day operations.

Types of Elementary and High School Districts

School District
A geographical unit created by the state to provide public education to the school-aged population within its boundaries.

The **school district** in which your school is located is a special unit of government. It has only one purpose—to provide education. In 2012, there were 424 school districts in Wisconsin.

In general, there are two types of school districts—common and unified (a special law applies only to the school district of Milwaukee).

Most districts operate full programs, ranging from preschool and kindergarten through 12th grade. In some cases, there are separate school districts for grades kindergarten through eight and a separate school district (called a union high school district) for grades nine through 12. The types of school districts differ in terms of organization and control. One difference involves who determines school policy.

How Have School Districts Changed?

During 1937-38, Wisconsin had 7,777 school districts. Of these, 6,181 were one-room school districts, and only 262 employed three or more teachers.

As the state became less rural, lawmakers placed new requirements on school districts and offered financial incentives to encourage school consolidations. External factors also played a role in school consolidations. For example, once school districts could provide motorized transportation, it was no longer necessary that children be within walking distance of a school.

By 1960, there were 826 school districts in Wisconsin. One-room schools disappeared by 1970. In 2012, there were 424 school districts.

Chapter Nine

Fort Atkinson High School students perform. (Photo courtesy of the Daily Jefferson County Union.)

Common and union high school districts operate very much alike, but union districts operate only high school grades nine through 12. Each is governed by a **school board** and holds an annual school meeting, which gives voters an opportunity to say how their schools should be run. The most important item of business usually is approval of the school taxes to be levied or the buying or selling of school property.

School Board
The governing body of a school district. It adopts the budget and sets overall policy for the district.

In unified school districts, general school operations are directed by an elected school board. They do not hold annual meetings. The school board adopts the school budget after a public hearing.

State law has special provisions for school districts in a "city of the first class" (defined by state statutes as having a population of 150,000 or more). In these cities a nine-member school board sets education policy, and adopts the school budget after a public hearing.

District Administrator
The individual responsible for the day-to-day operation of a school district.

The day-to-day operation of a school district is the responsibility of the **district administrator** or superintendent, who is hired by the school board.

9.2 FINANCING SCHOOLS

The school budget is an estimate of the amount of money that will be spent to operate the school district during the coming year. It also lists the amount of income, including state aid, that the school district expects to receive during the year. Figure 9.1 below shows how the typical school district spends money from its general fund. Figure 9.2 on page 117 shows where that money comes from.

School Property Tax Levy
The amount of money to be raised through property taxes in order to operate the school district.

The two main sources of school income are state aid (discussed earlier) and the property tax. The amount of money to be raised through property taxes is called the **school property tax levy**. School taxes are collected by towns, villages, and cities, and then turned over to school districts for school use. State law limits how much school districts can collect in property taxes and state aid.

The largest part of school general fund spending is for staff salaries and benefits, such as health insurance and pension contributions. Other important costs are utilities for building operation, supplies for maintenance and repair, transportation, and materials and technology for services such as libraries, guidance counseling, and data processing.

Referendum
A question or issue submitted directly to voters.

A school district may borrow money to build and equip new buildings. Often, it is necessary for the voters to approve a **referendum** authorizing the borrowing.

Figure 9.1
School General Fund Expenditure Dollar (2012)

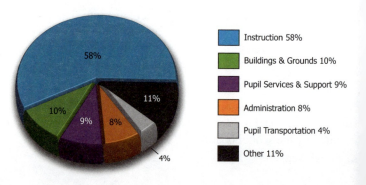

- Instruction 58%
- Buildings & Grounds 10%
- Pupil Services & Support 9%
- Administration 8%
- Pupil Transportation 4%
- Other 11%

9.3 ALTERNATIVES TO PUBLIC SCHOOLS

State law allows several alternatives to public schools. **Private schools**, operated by both nonprofit and for-profit groups, have long-played a major role in Wisconsin K-12 education. In 2011-12, over 12% of the state's elementary and secondary students attended private schools at their own expense, one of the largest percentages in the country. In the late 1960s, almost 25% of Wisconsin's K-12 students were enrolled in private schools. Many private schools are religious and provide religious instruction, which is prohibited in public schools.

State law also allows **home schooling,** in which families or groups of families teach their children at their own expense. Home schooling accounts for 1.9% of total state enrollment. Wisconsin is one of the least regulated states for home schoolers.

Still another alternative to public schools in some parts of Wisconsin are state-funded school vouchers, also known as **school choice.** Established in 1989, this program allows low-income parents to send their children, at public expense, to private schools. Pupils began attending private schools with vouchers in the 1990-91 school year.

The program began in Milwaukee. Initially, only nonreligious private schools could participate. In 1995, the state expanded the program to include sectarian (religious) schools, which survived a state supreme court challenge.

Private Schools
Schools that are established, conducted, and mainly supported by a non-governmental agency.

Home Schooling
An alternative to public school in which parents or groups of parents teach their own children at home.

Figure 9.2

School General Fund Revenue Dollar (2012)[1]

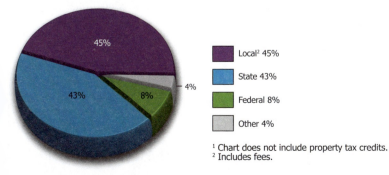

- Local[2] 45%
- State 43%
- Federal 8%
- Other 4%

[1] Chart does not include property tax credits.
[2] Includes fees.

School Choice
Generally refers to the ability of parents to choose the public or private school their children attend at public expense.

Open Enrollment
This program allows students to attend any public school in the state.

The U.S. Supreme Court has also ruled school choice constitutional. In the 2011-12 school year, over 23,000 part- and full-time pupils attended 106 private schools under the Milwaukee program. In 2011, the state expanded the school choice program to Racine. In 2011-12, eight private schools and 228 pupils there participated. In 2013, the program was expanded statewide.

Another state funded school option for families is open enrollment, which began in 1998-99. Under **open enrollment**, a student may attend any public school district in the state, provided the district has space and the transfer would not financially burden the student's home district or the host district. Transportation is not provided. In 2011-12, over 37,000 Wisconsin students participated in open enrollment. Some of these students attend "virtual schools" through online learning.

One of the fastest-growing alternatives to traditional public schools is the **charter school**. The Wisconsin Legislature created the charter school program in 1993 to offer public school students more opportunities, and to encourage innovation in public school instruction and organization.

Charter School
A publicly sponsored school that is exempt from many of the rules and regulations imposed on public schools under state law.

Charter schools are publicly sponsored and funded schools that are exempt from many of the rules and regulations traditionally mandated by state law. For example, charter schools are not required to provide physical education, art, or music instruction, nor are they required to provide guidance counseling, emergency nursing, or library media services. They can be sponsored by cities, public school districts, and colleges. State law does require charter schools to be free, public, and nonreligious. They must also comply with all federal laws and are held accountable for students' educational progress.

In 2011-12, Wisconsin's 232 charter schools were operating in 96 public school districts, offering nontraditional curricula and methods.

9.4 WISCONSIN TECHNICAL COLLEGE SYSTEM

In addition to school districts, the state is divided into 16 technical college districts (formerly called vocational, technical, and adult education, or VTAE districts). These districts

Chapter Nine   119

Fox Valley Technical College in Oshkosh. (Photo courtesy of Fox Valley Technical College.)

are much larger in area than a school district and most cover several counties. They are funded with a combination of student fees, state and federal aid, contract revenues, and property taxes.

Wisconsin was a pioneer in vocational education, establishing a separate vocational system in 1911. Early on, vocational programs were usually designed for people who had not finished high school and needed to learn a work skill.

Today's technical college districts offer a variety of educational and training courses for youth and adults. A person who did not complete high school may earn a high school diploma at a technical college. It is also possible to train for a trade or technical career, such as carpentry, nursing, electrical work, data processing, or automobile repair. In addition, there are opportunities to improve job skills or to pursue special interests, such as art or music.

Wisconsin technical colleges offer more than 300 programs, which include two-year associate degrees, one- and two-year technical diplomas, short-term (nine-month) technical certificates, and customized training for business and industry.

Each technical college district is governed by a nine-member board chosen by representatives from the general government units in the district. In many cases, the county board chairs jointly make appointments. By law, the board is made up of two employers and two employees who represent various businesses and industries in the district, three members of the general public, one elected state or local official, and one school district administrator. Some technical college boards are required to have a minority member based on the percentage of minority population in the district.

The district board has general control of the district's programs, employees, facilities, and finances. It selects a director to administer district affairs. Like local school boards, technical college district boards approve the annual budget and levy taxes. Technical colleges also may own property and assume debt.

At the state level, technical college districts are supervised by the Wisconsin Technical College System Board. The board consists of the following 13 members: the state superintendent of public instruction, the secretary of workforce development, and the president of the University of Wisconsin System, or their designees, as well as one employer, one employee, one farmer, one technical college student, and six additional members appointed by the governor and confirmed by the state senate. The board appoints a state director to handle the system's day-to-day operations. The board approves all construction, courses, and programs, and sets tuition for districts throughout the state. Wisconsin is unique in that it has a completely separate board to oversee technical education.

9.5 UNIVERSITY OF WISCONSIN SYSTEM

Prior to 1971, Wisconsin had two competing university systems—the University of Wisconsin and the Wisconsin State Universities System. A 1971 state law merged the two systems to form the University of Wisconsin (UW) System. The system includes 13 four-year institutions, known as universities, and 13 two-year campuses, known as colleges. In addition, UW-Extension provides learning opportunities for adults throughout the state.

The UW System is governed by an 18-member board of regents. The state superintendent of public instruction and the president of the technical college system are automatically appointed to the board. The 14 citizen members and two student members are appointed by the governor with senate consent. The student members are chosen through an application process and serve two-year terms. Other members serve seven-year terms.

The board of regents appoints the president of the UW System, the chancellors of the universities and the Extension, and the deans of the two-year UW colleges. All appointees serve at the pleasure of the board. The board also sets admission standards, reviews and approves university budgets, and establishes the regulatory framework of the system.

The UW System is led by the president, with the chancellors and deans of the two-year campuses and UW-Extension/Colleges reporting to the president.

REVIEW

Wisconsin's constitution requires the state to provide free public elementary and secondary (K-12) education to residents. In addition to the 424 K-12 school districts, Wisconsin also has 16 technical colleges, 13 public universities, and 13 two-year colleges that provide post-secondary education. ☐

Key Terms in This Chapter

- School Aids
- CESA
- School District
- School Board
- District Administrator
- School Property Tax Levy
- Referendum
- Private Schools
- Home Schooling
- School Choice
- Open Enrollment
- Charter School

10 Getting Involved

The actions of each unit of government in Wisconsin are based on what citizens want. The people are responsible for deciding what government should do, and they elect representatives to carry out their wishes. No matter your age, you can participate by attending meetings, writing your legislators, becoming active in a political party, working for a candidate for public office, or making a campaign contribution. At 18, you can vote and run for most offices.

IN THIS CHAPTER:

- 10.1 Wisconsin Government & You (123)
- 10.2 Politics: Democracy in Action (124)
- 10.3 A Continuum of Political Action (125)

10.1 WISCONSIN GOVERNMENT & YOU

As the story goes, when the Constitutional Convention of 1787 finished its work on a plan for a new American government, a Philadelphia woman, eager to know the results, approached Benjamin Franklin and asked: "Well, Doctor, what have we got, a republic or a monarchy?"

Franklin replied: "A republic, madam, if you can keep it."

And so began one of the world's oldest and longest experiments in self-government. Whether we can "keep" our republic is up to all of us, including you, just as it was up to our parents and grandparents, and their parents and grandparents.

Are you up to the task? What can you do to keep our republic healthy for another 200 years?

Above all, you need to know how our government works and learn about the important public issues it faces. You need to understand what taxes you pay, and how that money is used. That's why you study government in school and read books such as this.

But that's just the beginning. After all, in a democracy, *you* are the government. The people decide what government at all levels should do or not do. We do that by electing representatives—municipal officials, school board members, state lawmakers, and national leaders—and by making sure that those we elect know what we expect from them.

Even if you can't yet vote, you can influence the decisions government makes. You can talk to friends and neighbors.

> Freedom makes a huge requirement of every human being. With freedom comes responsibility. For the person who is unwilling to grow up, the person who does not want to carry his own weight, this is a frightening prospect.
>
> — Eleanor Roosevelt

You can write letters to newspaper editors. You can communicate with your elected officials. You can attend public meetings, or join a political party or interest group. You can encourage able people to run for office, as well as work for and contribute to candidates whom you support. Eventually, you can run for office yourself.

10.2 POLITICS: DEMOCRACY IN ACTION

Politics
The strategies employed by groups or individuals to gain power in government.

Some people don't like **politics**. They say it is dishonest, even dirty. But, actually, politics is only as good, or as bad, as you let it become.

Politics is nothing more than how we, individually and in groups, influence the choices and decisions our governments make. Politics is democracy in action—the way we get things done in government.

Getting things done in government is easier said than done. Individuals are not the same; their principles and priorities vary depending on many factors, including family background, occupation, place of residence, and even religion.

So, in a representative democracy, politics will almost always involve **compromise** among differing points of view.

Compromise
The process of differing sides making concessions in order to reach an agreement.

Compromise is necessary, not only in government, but also in organized political parties or interest groups, small neighborhood associations, informal gatherings of concerned citizens, and even families.

Consensus
An opinion held by all or most.

When disagreements arise, as they do, differences are resolved through informed discussion—and respectful listening to other points of view. Eventually, a compromise can be found that satisfies a majority of those involved. It is even better if **consensus**—a judgment shared by all those concerned—can be reached.

Without compromise or consensus, governments in our republic could not function. Sometimes, compromise produces a decision that few find ideal, but that most involved can accept.

If that is to happen and representative government is to thrive, it is important for all of us to participate in the political process.

> **Public Records Law**
>
> Unless access is denied by law, any requester has a right to inspect any state or local government record in Wisconsin.
>
> Record is defined in state law as "any material on which written, drawn, printed, spoken, visual, or electromagnetic information is recorded or preserved."
>
> Not every piece of paper or computer file is a public record. A draft document is not, for instance. If an authority denies a public records request, it must cite specific and sufficient reason for the denial.

Ordinary citizens are involved in Wisconsin government and influence its actions every day. They are most effective when they understand the issues being discussed and play an active role in the process. You, too, can take part in making the decisions and laws that affect us all. Good citizenship is not just a topic for study and politics is not a spectator sport, as often said. It requires active participation.

10.3 A CONTINUUM OF POLITICAL ACTION

President Lincoln understood this when, in 1863 at Gettysburg, he spoke of an American "government of the people, by the people, for the people, [that] shall not perish from the earth." What he really was saying in this famous speech was that freedom requires responsibility.

All citizens must work together to preserve our American freedoms. Political involvement takes many forms, ranging from doing nothing to engaging in civil disobedience (see Figure 10.1 on pages 126 and 127). Think of it as a continuum. All the actions described on the following pages are part of this country's history, but only those actions that require some kind of positive involvement contribute to "keeping" our republic, as Franklin urged.

Apathy

Unfortunately, the first, and sadly, most common form of political behavior in which people engage is inaction. **Apathy,** or an unwillingness to get involved at any level on any issue, is used to describe this lack of involvement. Apathetic

Apathy
An unwillingness to get involved.

people ignore politics, government, and the issues at hand for a variety of reasons including laziness, fear, and ignorance.

Casting an Informed Vote

To be an informed voter, it is important to follow political events and candidates and to develop an opinion. You do this by learning about government actions and issues in newspapers and magazines, on radio or television, or on credible websites.

It is wise to get news from a variety of sources, including television, radio, newspapers, and the Internet. Look for sources known for providing balanced and accurate information. Sometimes, blogs and other online sources are written by those who use information carelessly to voice half-truths and biased opinions. Established news outlets with ethical journalists and professional standards can often be most reliable.

Figure 10.1
A Continuum of Political Action

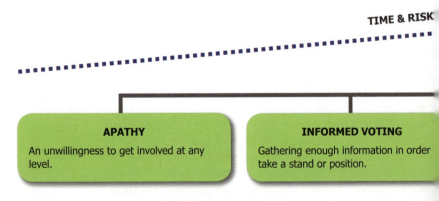

APATHY
An unwillingness to get involved at any level.

INFORMED VOTING
Gathering enough information in order take a stand or position.

*As you move up this continuum, the amount of time and/or risk increases. The options at far right involve actions that can be illegal, even revolutionary.

Even better, read information provided directly by candidates and government officials; evaluate its accuracy, and compare it with information from others with opposing views. However you choose to stay informed, study and analyze the positions of political candidates and cast your ballot based on those positions.

When you turn 18, you can do more than support candidates or express opinions, you can vote. When that time comes, contact your city, town, or village clerk and register to vote. You don't have to wait until election day. To register by mail, the deadline is 5 p.m. on the (20th day) third Wednesday before an election. To register in person, go to the clerk's office no later than the Friday before an election. In Wisconsin, you can also register at the polls with acceptable proof of residence, but understand that this method can involve patience and waiting. For more information on registering

DIRECT ACTION
- Communicate with elected officials
- Support a political action committee (PAC), special interest group, political candidate, or political party.
- Join a political party or a special interest group.
- Become directly involved to help draw attention to an issue or a candidate.
- Run for elected office.

DISOBEDIENCE
- Nonviolent civil disobedience.
- Violent action.
- Revolution.

to vote, go to http://gab.wi.gov/elections-voting/voters/registration-voting.

Taking Direct Action

Other than voting, there are a number of other ways to be politically active.

You can influence government decisionmakers and elected officials by writing letters, sending emails, making phone calls, or signing petitions. Don't ever underestimate the impact a few motivated **constituents** can have.

> **Constituents**
> The people of an area or district represented by a public official.

You can also support a political action committee (PAC), special interest group, political candidate, or political party. You can do this by contributing time or money to a party, candidate, or group that favors your positions on issues. Be aware that in Wisconsin, there are limits to how much money you can give to candidates.

You can go one step further and formally join a political party or interest group that reflects your views. This often involves paying dues, attending meetings, or working on committees.

Finally, you can become active by attending marches, rallies, or demonstrations; distributing informative literature; speaking in public; and circulating petitions. Any of these actions encourage others to become involved by drawing attention to an issue or candidate.

Run for Office

Once you are 18, not only can you vote, you can also run for most elective offices. You first have to take the necessary steps to register as a candidate and have your name placed on the ballot. As a candidate, you will then develop issue positions, find supporters, and raise money to educate voters about you and your ideas. If elected, you will attend regular meetings, listen to constituents, and take responsibility for making decisions on behalf of the people you serve.

Public service is not always easy. At times, it can involve sacrificing money, personal and family time, and even privacy. You also lose your ability to blame others for what government

> **It's never too early to get involved!**
>
> **Q.** Who was the youngest person ever to serve in the Wisconsin Assembly?
>
> **A.** Michael Elconin (D-Milwaukee) was first elected in 1972 at the age of 19. He won the 1972 election 11,457 to 2,739. He served in 1973-74, 1975-76, and 1977-78.
>
> Note: In 1988, at the age of 17, Neil Willenson was the youngest person ever to run for the Wisconsin Assembly. His birthday was in December, so he would have been 18 when sworn-in. He was the Democratic candidate in the 58th Assembly District. He lost the election (7,165 to 18,367) to Stephen Loucks (R-Mequon).

is doing. But, win or lose, running for office is the ultimate act of citizenship. There is no better way to influence political decisionmaking.

You might, at times, be criticized by opponents and blamed unfairly for problems people think you caused. But, when your term of office is over, you will have made a needed and vital contribution to preserving self-government. You might even receive thanks from grateful citizens who understand the fundamental importance of public involvement and public service.

There's no time like now to become involved. Wisconsin has seen a number of young people elected as mayors in cities throughout the state. These include:

- Matt Harter, age 24, La Crosse (2009);
- Justin Nichols, age 22, Manitowoc (2010);
- Romaine Quinn, age 19, Rice Lake (2010); and
- Zach Vruwink, age 24, Wisconsin Rapids (2012).

Civil Disobedience

There are times when people feel so strongly about a public issue or government action that they find it necessary to engage in **civil disobedience** in order to demand change in a law, or even in an entire government. At various times in our history, civil disobedience has involved refusing to pay taxes,

Civil Disobedience
Refusal to obey governmental rules and laws as a form of protest.

obstructing traffic or blocking entrances to public buildings, conducting sit-ins in government offices, and defying court orders. To be clear: These can be illegal acts for which people are arrested.

In the tradition of Gandhi in India and the Rev. Martin Luther King Jr. in the United States, civil disobedience in modern times has generally been nonviolent, even when illegal.

When actions go further and involve destruction of property or injuring people, protests become violent. Whether such actions can be defended or justified in a democratic society governed by laws is hotly debated. Two hundred years ago, during a time of monarchical rule from afar, American colonists obviously felt that violent rebellion was necessary.

If all U.S. citizens work actively to exercise our rights and protect our freedoms, we help ensure that we "keep" our republic as the nation's founders envisioned. Extensive citizen involvement in government is an important antidote to violent action and to the injury it can do to self-government.

REVIEW

It is not enough to learn about the workings of government at all levels. In order to strengthen our democracy, it is important that we participate in it. At a minimum, we can all stay informed on the challenging issues that confront us at the local, state, and national levels. And we can use the insights we gain from that process to make informed choices on election day. □

Key Terms in This Chapter

- Politics
- Compromise
- Consensus
- Apathy
- Constituents
- Civil Disobedience

Selected Resources

Buenker, John D. *The History of Wisconsin: The Progressive Era, 1893-1914.* Madison: State Historical Society of Wisconsin, 1998.

Buenker, John D. "Wisconsin as Maverick, Model, and Microcosm." In *Heartland: Comparative Histories of the Midwestern States,* ed. James H. Madison, Bloomington: Indiana University Press, 1988.

Crane, Wilder, and Clark A. Hagensick, eds. Wisconsin Government and Politics. New York, N.Y.

Nesbit, Robert C., and William F. Thompson. *Wisconsin: A History.* Madison: University of Wisconsin Press, 1989.

Risjord, Norman K. *Wisconsin: The Story of the Badger State.* Madison: Trails Book, 2007.

Smith, Alice E. *The History of Wisconsin: From Exploration to Statehood.* Madison: State Historical Society of Wisconsin, 1973.

Thompson, William F. *The History of Wisconsin: Continuity and Change, 1940-1965.* Madison: State Historical Society of Wisconsin, 2013.

Wisconsin Legislative Reference Bureau, comp. State of Wisconsin Blue Book 2011-2012. Madison: Author, 2011.

Douglas County Historical Society (www.douglashistory.org).

League of Wisconsin Municipalities (www.lwm-info.org).

State Elections Board (http://gab.wi.gov/).

State of Wisconsin (www.wisconsin.gov).

U.S. Census Bureau (www.census.gov).

University of Wisconsin System (www.wisconsin.edu).

Wisconsin Bar Association (www.wisbar.org).

Wisconsin Counties Association (www.wicounties.org).

Wisconsin Department of Administration (http://doa.wi.gov/).

Wisconsin Department of Natural Resources (http://dnr.wi.gov).

Wisconsin Department of Public Instruction (http://dpi.wi.gov/).

Wisconsin Department of Transportation (http://www.dot.wisconsin.gov/).

Wisconsin Department of Workforce Development (http://www.dwd.state.wi.us/).

Wisconsin Historical Society (www.wisconsinhistory.org).

Wisconsin Legislative Reference Bureau (http://www.legis.state.wi.us/lrb).

Wisconsin State Legislature (www.legis.state.wi.us).

Wisconsin Supreme Court (www.wicourts.gov).

Wisconsin Towns Association (www.wisctowns.com). ☐

Index

Abrahamson, Shirley S. 52
Acts 38
Administrative agencies 45, 46
Administrative coordinator 79
Administrator 93
Advisory referendum 28
African Americans 5
Agribusiness 11
Aids to individuals 68
Aldermanic districts 89
Alderpersons 89
America's Dairyland 10
Anishinabe 5
Annexation 88
Annual town meeting 106
Apathy 125
Appellate court 53, 54
Appellate jurisdiction 53
Assembly 34
Assessor 109
Attorney general 47, 48

Barca, Peter 38
Bayfield 89
Board of trustees 89
Biennium 61
Biennial session 35
Bills 38
Bonds 66
Boroughs 75
British 5, 11

California 6, 9
Casting an informed vote 126
Casting your vote 26, 27
Charter 90, 92
Charter school 118
Chief justice 54
Cities 87
City assessor 90
City attorney 90
City budget 94, 95
City engineer 90
City clerk 90
City of first class 115
City treasurer 90
Civil case 52
Civil disobedience 129

Clerk of circuit court 80
Closed primary 21
Common council 89
Common Man 13
Common school district 114
Compromise 124
Concurrence 39
Concurrent jurisdiction 53
Conference committee 41
Consensus 124
Constituents 128
Constitutional amendment 32
Constitutional convention 32
Constitutional Convention of 1787 123
Continuum of political action 125-127
Cooperative Education Service Agency (CESA) 18, 113, 114
Coroner 80, 84
Coroner's jury 56
Corporate income tax 64
Council-manager form 91
Counties 75
County administrator 79, 80
County board of supervisors 79, 81
County clerk 77, 80, 81
County executive 79, 80
County expenditure dollar 82
County Highway Department 77
County income dollar 83
County register of deeds 77, 80
County sales tax 84
County sheriff 77, 80, 83
County treasurer 80, 81
Criminal case 52
Croatians 5
Czechs 5

Democratic Party 21
Democrats 12, 13
Department of Administration (DOA) 49, 87, 88
Department of Agriculture, Trade and Consumer Protection (DATCP) 49
Department of Children and Families (DCF) 49
Department of Commerce 51
Department of Corrections (DOC) 50
Department of Employee Trust Funds 51
Department of Financial Institutions 51
Department of Justice 51

Department of Health Services (DHS) 50, 67
Department of Military Affairs 51
Department of Natural Resources (DNR) 50
Department of Public Instruction (DPI) 50, 67
Department of Revenue (DOR) 51, 62
Department of Safety and Professional Services 51
Department of Tourism 51
Department of Transportation (DOT) 51, 67
Department of Veterans Affairs 51
Department of Workforce Development (DWD) 51
Direct democracy 107, 108
District administrator 115
District attorney 77, 80, 84
Dutch 10

Economy 7
Elconin, Michael 129
Era of Progressive Reform 15
Excise tax 65
Exclusive jurisdiction 53
Executive branch 33, 34, 45-51
Expenditures 67

Federal aid 66, 96
Fiscal year 61
Flow of revenues and expenditures 69
Food stamp benefits 82
Franklin, Benjamin 123

Gandhi 130
General election 21, 22
General purpose revenue (GPR) 61, 65,
Germantown 104
Germans 5, 10, 15
Germany 14
Gold rush 1849 9
Governor 45
Government reform 15
Grand jury 56
Greeks 5
Green Bay 92
Green Party 21

Harter, Matt 129
Health and human services 82
Ho-Chunk 5
Home-rule 78, 90, 92
Home schooling 117
How a bill becomes law 40
How cases reach the State Supreme Court 55

Hungarians 5

Illinois 11
Immigrants 5, 14
Incorporate 87
Incorporation 88
Incorporation Review Board 88
Indiana 11
Individual income tax 64
Insurance premiums tax 65
Interest groups 24, 25
Irish 5
Italians 5

Jackson, Andrew 12
Jacksonian Era 13
Jacksonian Democracy 12
Joint committee on finance 37, 62
Judicial branch 33, 34, 52-58
Juries 56
Jurisdiction 52, 53

Kenosha County 7
King Jr., Rev. Martin Luther 130

La Follette, Robert M. "Fighting Bob" 15
Land Cessions Treaty of 1837 (Pine Tree Treaty) 8
Legislative branch 33, 34
Legislative Fiscal Bureau (LFB) 62
Libertarian Party 21
Lieutenant governor 46, 47
Lobbyist 24, 25
Local aids 68

Majority leader 36
Mandate 70
Manufacturing 11
Marathon County 76, 77
Mayor 89, 90
Mayor-council form (strong) 91, 92
Mayor-council form (weak) 91, 92
Medicaid 66, 68, 77
Medical examiner 80
Menominee County 76, 77, 79, 103
Menominee County board 79
Michigan 11
Michigan Territory 8, 103
Milwaukee 15, 89, 92
Milwaukee County 7, 76, 77, 78, 79, 80, 106
Minnesota 6

Minority leader 36
Miscellaneous taxes 65
Municipal courts 57, 58
Municipal judge 89

Native American peoples 5, 8
Negro suffrage 13
New York 13
New Yorkers 10
News media 26
Nichols, Justin 129
Nonconcurrence 39, 41
Nonfiscal items 70
Nonpartisan elections 22
Nonpartisan offices 23
Northwest Ordinance of 1787 11
Northwest Territories 11, 14
Norway 14
Norwegians 5, 15

Ojibwe (Ojibway, Ojibwa) 5, 7, 8
Ohio 11
Open enrollment 118
Open meeting law 48
Open primary 21
Ordinances 90
Original jurisdiction 53

Parishes 75
Partial veto 42
Partisan 21
Partisan offices 23
Party caucus 35, 36
Pepin County 76, 77
Petit jury 56
Pine Tree Treaty 8
Political action committee (PAC) 128
Political parties 21
Polk, James K. 12
Politics 124
Potawatomi 5
President of the senate 35
President of the University of Wisconsin System 120
President pro tempore 35
Primary election 22, 24
Private schools 117
Program revenues 65, 66
Progressive Era 16
Progressives 15, 16

Property tax 96
Property tax bill 97
Property tax levy 96
Property tax rate 98
Public records law 125
Public utility tax 65

Quinn, Romaine 129

Racine county 7
Redistrict 34
Referendum 116
Relationship of state and federal courts 57
Representative government 87
Republican Party 15, 16, 21
Register to vote 127
Reserved powers 31
Revenue 63
Revolutionary War 11
Roosevelt, Eleanor 123
Run for office 128
Russians 5

Sales tax 64
Sauk 5
Scandinavians 5, 10
School aids 113
School board 115
School choice 117, 118
School districts 113, 114
School property tax levy 116
School vouchers 117
Secretary of state 47
Secretary of Workforce Development 120
Segregated revenues 65
Senate 34
Serbians 5
Sewer socialists 15
Shires 75
Sioux 8
Slovaks 5
Social Democrat 16
Social Gospel Movement 15
Socialist 16
Speaker of the assembly 35
Speaker pro tempore 35
Special interest group 128
Special interests 25
Special purpose districts 18
Stalwarts 15

State aid 68, 96
State budget 46, 61
State budget cycle 63
State constitution 31
State departments 49
State government agencies 48
State open meeting law 95
State spending by purpose 68
State spending from all revenue sources 71
State superintendent of public instruction 48, 113, 120, 121
State treasurer 47
Subsistence agriculture 7
Suffrage 13
Swiss 10

Thailand 6
Three branches of Wisconsin government 33
Tourism 10
Town 103
Town assessor 108, 109
Town board of supervisors 106, 107
Town chair 108
Town clerk 108
Town constable 108
Town expenditure dollar 109
Town income dollar 108
Town meeting 106, 107
Town supervisors 108
Town treasurer 108, 109
Treaty 8
Treaty of Cedars of 1836 8
Treaty of Paris 11
Types of city government 91
Types of elementary and high school districts 114
Types of jurisdiction 53

Unfunded mandates 83
Unified school district 114, 115
Unincorporated villages 105, 106
Union high school district 114
Units of government 17
University of Wisconsin 16
University of Wisconsin System 67, 120, 121
U.S. Bill of Rights 33
U.S. Constitution 31
UW-Extension 120, 121
Utility district 105

Veto 42
Vietnam War 6
Village assessor 89
Village budget 95
Village of Bellevue 88
Village of Caledonia 88
Village clerk 89
Village constable 89
Village of Hobart 88
Village of Kronenwetter 88
Village of Lake Hallie 88
Village of Menomonee Falls 88
Village of Suamico 88
Village of Summit 88
Village treasurer 89
Villages 87
Virtual schools 118
Vocational, technical, and adult education (VTAE districts) 118
Vos, Robin 38
Vote buying 25
Voter registration 27
Voter turnout 27, 28
Vruwink, Zach 129

Waukesha County 7
Wisconsin Act 171 87
Wisconsin circuit courts 56, 57
Wisconsin Constitution 12, 31, 34, 52, 78, 87
Wisconsin counties map 76
Wisconsin court of appeals 55
Wisconsin Declaration of Rights 32, 33
Wisconsin Economic Development Corporation 51
Wisconsin Idea 16
Wisconsin legislator annual salary 35
Wisconsin Progressives 15
Wisconsin statutes 39
Wisconsin Supreme Court 52-54
Wisconsin Technical College System 118
Wisconsin Technical College System Board 120
Wood county 17

Yankees 5, 13
York 104